Twilight Los Angeles, 1992

Also by Anna Deavere Smith available from
Anchor Books

Fires in the Mirror:
Crown Heights, Brooklyn, and Other Identities

Anchor Books

A Division of Random House, Inc.

New York

Twilight Los Angeles, 1992 On the Road:

A Search for American Character

Anna Deavere Smith

First Anchor Books Edition, April 1994

Library of Congress Cataloging-in-Publication Data

Smith, Anna Deavere.
  Twilight—Los Angeles, 1992 : on the road : a search for American character / Anna Deavere Smith.
      p.   cm.
    1. Los Angeles (Calif.)—Social conditions—Drama.   2. Los Angeles (Calif.)—Race relations—Drama.   3. Riots—California—Los Angeles—Drama.   I. Title.
PS3569.M465T95   1994
812'.54—dc20   93-38298
                                                                              CIP

ISBN 0-385-47375-3
ISBN 0-385-47376-1 (Pbk.)

Book design by Gretchen Achilles

www.anchorbooks.com

Printed in the United States of America
19   18

This book is dedicated to the
citizens of Los Angeles.

Contents

PROLOGUE

THE TERRITORY

HERE'S A NOBODY

WAR ZONE

The Park Family

TWILIGHT

JUSTICE

Acknowledgments

Gordon Davidson, George Wolfe, Stanley Sheinbaum, Betty Sheinbaum, Merry Conway.

Stanford University Department of Drama, Michael Ramsaur, Irvine Foundation, Rockefeller Study and Conference Center in Bellagio, Italy, Suzanne Sato, Susan Garfield.

Elizabeth Alexander, Theresa Allison, Kathy Cho, Eisa Davis, Thulani Davis, Robert Egan, Oskar Eustis, Jose Manuel Galvan, Roberta Goodman, Kishisha Jefferson, Dorinne Kondo, Kyung-Ja Lee, June K. Lu, Jamie Lyons, Emily Mann, Rosamaria Marquez, Irene Mecchi, Angela Oh, Alice Raynor, Jack Tantleff, Rosemarie Tischler, Hector Tobar, Richard Yarborough, Nancy Yoo, Peter Zeisler.

I also would like to express my deep gratitude to Cecelia Pang for her care and maintenance of the written text in various stages of its development.

Additionally, I am indebted to all of the people who granted me interviews in the course of my research in Los Angeles.

Introduction

In May 1992 I was commissioned by Gordon Davidson, artistic director/producer of the Mark Taper Forum in Los Angeles, to create a one-woman performance piece about the civil disturbances in that city in April 1992. For over ten years now I have been creating performances based on actual events in a series I have titled *On the Road: A Search for American Character*. Each *On the Road* performance evolves from interviews I conduct with individuals directly or indirectly involved in the event I intend to explore. Basing my scripts entirely on this interview material, I perform the interviewees on stage using their own words. *Twilight: Los Angeles, 1992* is the product of my search for the character of Los Angeles in the wake of the initial Rodney King verdict.

In the course of my research for the play I interviewed about two hundred people. Due to time restrictions, however, the number of people I was able to portray on stage was limited to about twenty-five. This book includes some of the material I performed both in the play's Los Angeles version for the Taper and in the version presented at the New York Shakespeare Festival. It includes additional interviews that were not included in the stage versions, which I hope will enrich the reader's understanding of the conflicts that erupted on April 29, 1992. For those who both see the play and read the book, I hope the book can serve as a companion to the theater experience.

The story of how Los Angeles came to experience what some call the worst riots in United States history is by now familiar. In the Spring of 1991, Rodney King, a black man, was severely beaten by four white Los Angeles police officers after a high-speed chase in which King was pursued for speeding. A nearby resident videotaped the beating from the balcony of his apartment. When the videotape was broadcast on national television, there was an immediate outcry from the community. The next year, the police officers who beat King were tried and found not guilty—and the city exploded. The verdict took the city by surprise, from public officials to average citizens. Even the defense lawyers, I was told, anticipated that there would be some convictions. Three days of burning, looting, and killing scarred Los Angeles and captured the attention of the world.

That is the extent of what most Americans understand to have caused what, depending on your point of view, would be variously referred to as a "riot," an "uprising," and/or a "rebellion." But beneath this surface explanation is a sea of associated causes. The worsening California economy and the deterioration of social services and public education in Los Angeles certainly paved the way to unrest. In 1968 President Lyndon Johnson convened the Kerner Commission to examine the causes of riots that shook more than 150 American cities in 1967. The commission's report highlighted urban ills and the plight of the urban poor. Yet more than twenty years later, living conditions for blacks and Latinos in Los Angeles have hardly improved, and Rodney King's beating was only the most visible example of years of police brutality toward people of color. The Watts riots, for example, were sparked by an altercation between a black man and the LAPD. In a speech given at the First African Methodist Episcopal Church in Los Angeles, California Congresswoman Maxine Waters spoke vividly about the legacy of the Watts riots:

There was an insurrection in this city before,
and, if I remember correctly,
it was sparked by police brutality.
We had a Kerner Commission report.
It talked about what was wrong with our society.
It talked about institutionalized racism.
It talked about a lack of services,
lack of government responsiveness to the people.
Today,
as we stand here in 1992,
if you go back and read the report,
it seems as though we are talking about what that report
    cited
some twenty years ago,
still exists today.

The police officers who beat Rodney King were tried in Simi Valley, miles away from the social, economic, and racial problems in Los Angeles. More important, they were miles away from what many residents of the epicenter of the riots, South-Central L.A., would call a war between residents and police officers. When I visited the quiet, predominantly white suburban community of Simi Valley, I began to perceive how profoundly different our experiences of law enforcement can be. For jurors in Simi Valley, Rodney King appeared to be a threat to the police. Moreover, he had been speeding. The officers were, as far as they were concerned, enforcing the law. Police officers reportedly concluded that King was on the drug PCP, impervious to pain, and therefore not responding to the beating. On the other hand, when I interviewed Rodney King's aunt, she burst into tears as she recounted seeing the beating on television, and "hearing him holler." She heard King's cries the first time she saw the tape. Yet a juror in the federal civil rights trial against the officers who also heard King's reaction to the police blows told me that the rest of the jury had difficulty hearing what she and King's aunt had heard. But when, during deliberations, they focused on the audio rather than the video image, their perspective changed. The physical image of Rodney King had to be taken away for them to agree that he was in pain and responding to the beating.

Although I did not attend the original trial in Simi Valley, I did attend the subsequent federal civil rights trial. There, I was able to imagine how such a jury could become convinced that, although the beating seemed brutal to any layman, it was, according to the defense, within the guidelines of the LAPD use-of-force policy. Moreover, I came to observe that some people are effected by the power of what District Attorney Gil Garcetti would describe as the "aura" and "magic" of the police, especially when police officers come to court. There they appeared polite, well groomed, and ready to "protect and serve." This image differed radically from the image of police conveyed to me by Michael Zinzun, a community activist and chairperson of the South-Central-based Coalition Against Police Abuse. The walls of his office were covered with blown-up photographs of people who had been beaten by police—bruised, bloodied, maimed. Zinzun himself had won a case against the city because he had been blinded when he attempted to intervene in a police beating of someone in his community.

The video of the Rodney King beating, which seemed to "tell all," apparently did not tell enough, and the prosecution lost, as their lead attorney told me, "the slam-dunk case of the century." The city of Los Angeles lost much more. *Twilight* is an attempt to explore the shades of that loss. It is not really an attempt to find causes or to show where responsibility was lacking. That would be the task of a commission report. While I was in Los Angeles, and when I have returned since my initial performance of *Twilight* in the summer of 1993, I have been trying to look at the shifts in attitudes of citizens toward race relations. I have been particularly interested in the opportunity the events in Los Angeles give us to take stock of how the race canvas in America has *changed* since the Watts riots. Los Angeles shows us that the story of race in America is much larger and more complex than a story of black and white. There are new players in the race drama. Whereas Jewish merchants were hit during the Watts riots, Korean merchants were hit this time. Although the media tended to focus on blacks in South-Central, the Latino population was equally involved. We tend to think of race as us and them—us or them being black or white depending on one's own color. The relationships among peoples of color and *within* racial groups are getting more and more complicated.

Where does theater fit into this? Theater can mirror society. But in order to do that theater must embrace diversity. It must include new characters in our human drama that have not been portrayed on our stages. Clearly even white mainstream theater could be more interesting, and more honest, if people of color were integrated into the drama rather than used as walk-on stereotypes. We now have the opportunity to be a part of the discovery of a larger, healthier, more interesting picture of America. I went to Los Angeles as part of this process, to listen to those who had lived through the disturbances and to reiterate their voices in the theater. I have felt in this project, more than once, an increased humility, and a greater understanding of the limitations of theater to reflect society. In developing the *On the Road* project, it was my goal to develop a kind of theater that could be more sensitive to the events of my own time than traditional theater could. This book is a part of that quest.

The challenge of creating *On the Road* works is to select the voices that best represent the event I hope to portray. *Twilight* was a particular challenge in this regard due to the number and the diversity of the voices I had gathered through interviews. I had made decisions as to which interviews to include on my own. However, since *Fires in the Mirror*, I have found it helpful to include more people in the creative process. I developed *Twilight* at the Mark Taper Forum in collaboration with four other people of various races who functioned as dramaturges (a dramaturge is a person who assists in the preparation of the text of a play and can offer an outside perspective to those who are more active in the process of staging the play). These dramaturges brought their own real-world experiences with race to bear on the work. They reacted to *Twilight* at every stage of its development.

My predominant concern about the creation of *Twilight* was that my own history, which is a history of race as a black and white struggle, would make the work narrower than it should be. For this reason, I sought out dramaturges who had very developed careers and identities, outside the theater profession. I was interested not only in their ethnic diversity, but in the diversity that they would bring to the project in terms of areas of expertise. I am a strong critic of the insularity of people in theater and of our inability to shake up our traditions, particularly with regard to race and representation issues. An issue that is at the heart of many theater conferences and gatherings is the need to make theater a more responsible partner in the growth of communities.

Among the people I asked to join me were Dorinne Kondo, a Japanese American anthropologist and feminist scholar; Hector Tobar, a Guatemalan-American reporter from the *Los Angeles Times* who had covered the riots; and the African American poet and University of Chicago professor Elizabeth Alexander. Oskar Eustis, a resident director at the Taper, also joined the dramaturgical team.

After every performance during previews, I met with the dramaturges and with the director and members of the staff of the Taper. Many of the meetings were very emotional. They were dramas in and of themselves. The most outspoken members of the group were Dorinne and Hector. They passionately attacked the black-and-white canvas that most of us in the room were inclined to perpetuate.

After my work at the Taper, and in revising the text for the New York production, I went to the Rockefeller Foundation's Study and Conference Center in Bellagio, Italy, to work with my acting coach, Merry Conway, who has been working with me at various times during the development of *On the Road* since its beginnings. The bottom line of my choice in material for a text is what happens when I actually *act* the material. Merry and I worked on a lot of material that never appeared in the play in any production, but which does appear in this book. What most influences my decisions about what to include is how an interview text works as a *physical, audible, performable* vehicle. Words are not an end in themselves. They are a means to evoking the character of the person who spoke them. Every person that I include in the book, and who I perform, has a presence that is much more important than the information they give.

This book is first and foremost a document of what an *actress heard* in Los Angeles. The performance is a reiteration of that. When I did my research in Los Angeles, I was listening with an ear that was trained to hear stories for the specific purpose of repeating them with the elements of character intact. This becomes significant because sometimes there is the expectation that inasmuch as I am doing "social dramas," I am looking for *solutions* to social problems. In fact, though, I am looking at the *processes* of the problems. Acting is a constant process of becoming something. It is not a result, it is not an answer. It is not a solution. I am first looking for the humanness inside the problems, or the crises. The spoken word is evidence of the humanness. Perhaps the solutions come somewhere further down the road.

I see the work as a call. I played *Twilight* in Los Angeles as a call to the community. I performed it at a time when the community had not yet resolved the problems. I wanted to be a part of their examination of the problems. I believe that solutions to these problems will call for the participation of large and eclectic groups of people. I also believe that we are at a stage at which we must first break the silence about race and encourage many more people to participate in the dialogue.

One of the questions I was frequently asked when I was interviewed about *Twilight* was "Did you find any one voice that could speak for the entire city?" I think there is an expectation that in this diverse city, and in this diverse nation, a unifying voice would bring increased understanding and put us on the road to solutions. This expectation surprises me. There is little in culture or education that encourages the development of a unifying voice. In order to have real unity, all voices would have to first be heard or at least represented. Many of us who work in race relations do so from the point of view of our own ethnicity. This very fact inhibits our ability to hear more voices than those that are closest to us in proximity. Few people speak a language about race that is not their own. If more of us could actually speak from another point of view, like speaking another language, we could accelerate the flow of ideas.

The boundaries of ethnicity do yield brilliant work. In some cases these boundaries provide safer places that allow us to work in atmospheres where we are supported and can support the works of others. In some cases it's very exciting to work with like-minded people in similar fields of interest. In other cases these boundaries have been crucial to the development of identity and the only conceivable response to a popular culture and a mainstream that denied the possibility of the development of identity. On the other hand the price we pay is that few of us can really look at the story of race in its complexity and its scope. If we were able to move more frequently beyond these boundaries, we would develop multifaceted identities and we would develop a more complex language. After all, identity is in some ways a process toward character. It is not character itself. It is not fixed. Our race dialogue desperately needs this more complex language. The words of Twilight, the ex–gang member after whom I named the play, addresses this need:

Twilight is that time of day between day and night
limbo, I call it limbo,
and sometimes when I take my ideas to my homeboys

they say, well Twilight, that's something you can't do right
    now,
that's an idea before its time.
So sometimes I feel as though I'm stuck in limbo
the way the sun is stuck between night and day
in the twilight hours.
Nighttime to me is like a lack of sun,
but I don't affiliate darkness with anything negative.
I affiliate darkness with what came first,
because it was first,
and relative to my complexion,
I am a dark individual
and with me being stuck in limbo
I see the darkness as myself.
And I see the light as the knowledge and the wisdom of the
    world, and the understanding of others.
And I know
that in order for me to be a full human being
I cannot forever dwell in darkness
I cannot forever dwell in idea
of identifying with those like me
and understanding only me and mine.

Twilight's recognition that we must reach across ethnic boundaries is simple but true.

Production History

Twilight: Los Angeles, 1992 was conceived, written, and performed by Anna Deavere Smith. It was originally produced by the Center Theatre Group/Mark Taper Forum in Los Angeles: Gordon Davidson, artistic director/producer, and Emily Mann, director.

It premiered on May 23, 1993, and closed on July 18, 1993. It was subsequently produced as a work in progress at the McCarter Theatre in Princeton, New Jersey.

Twilight's original New York production was provided by the New York Shakespeare Festival, George C. Wolfe, producer.

It opened at the New York Shakespeare Festival in March 1994 and was directed by George C. Wolfe.

All material is taken from interviews conducted by Anna Deavere Smith.

At the Mark Taper Forum, Charles Dillingham served as managing director and Robert Egan as producing director. Robert Brill designed the set; Candice Donnelly, the costumes; Allen Lee Hughes, the lighting; Lucia Hwong, the original music score; Jon Gottlieb, the sound; Jon Stolzberg of Intelewall, the multimedia design; and Merry Conway, the physical dramaturgy. Dramaturges: Elizabeth Alexander, Oskar Eustis, Dorinne Kondo, and Hector Tobar. Corey Beth Madden was associate producer; Ed De Shae, production stage manager; and Richard Hollabaugh, stage manager. Cecilia J. Pang was assistant to Anna Deavere Smith; Kishisha Jefferson, field assistant to Anna Deavere Smith; Eisa Davis, assistant to Emily Mann; Thulani Davis, workshop dramaturge; Jamie Lyons, Stanford University student intern; and Kathy Cho and Nancy Yoo, research assistants.

At the New York Shakespeare Festival Tony Kushner was dramaturge; John Arnone designed the scenery; Jules Fisher and Peggy Eisenhauer, the lighting; John Gromada, the sound. At press time, the selection of the creative team was incomplete.

Twilight: Los Angeles, 1992 is part of a series of solo pieces created and performed by Anna Deavere Smith called *On the Road: A Search for American Character.*

Prologue

My Enemy
Rudy Salas, Sr. Sculptor and painter

(A large very warm man, with a blue shirt with the tails out and blue jeans and tennis shoes. He is at a dining-room table with a white tablecloth. There is a bank of photographs in frames on the sideboard next to the table. There is a vase of flowers on another table near the table. There are paintings of his on the wall. Nearest the table is a painting of his wife. His wife, Margaret, a woman in glasses and a long flowered dress, moves around the room. For a while she takes photo albums out of the sideboard and out of the back room, occasionally saying something. She is listening to the entire interview. He has a hearing aid in his left ear and in his right ear. He is sitting in a wooden captain's chair, medium-sized. He moves a lot in the chair, sometimes with his feet behind the front legs, and his arms hanging over the back of the chair. He is very warm.)

An then my
my grandfather,
N. Carnación,
uh,
was a
gringo hater
'cause he had run-ins with gringos
when he was riding.
He had been a rebel,
so see there was another twist—
he had rode with Villa and those people and he remembers
    when he

fought the gringos when they went into Chihuahua
Pershing went in there to chase Villa and all that?
So I grew up with all this rich stuff at home,
(*Three quick hits on the table and a double sweep*)
and then at school,
first grade, they started telling me
I was inferior
because I was a Mexican,
and that's where
(*He hits the table several times, taps, twenty-three taps until
line "the enemy" and then on "nice white teachers" his hand
sweeps the table*)
I realized I had an enemy
and that enemy was those nice white teachers.
I wonder what is it,
why
did I have this madness
that I understood this?
It's not an enemy I hated.
It's not a hate thing,
the insanity that I carried with me started when I took the
    beating
from the police.
Okay, that's where the insanity came in.
In forty-
two,
when I was in my teens
running around as a zoot-suiter,
one night the cop really tore me up bad.
I turned around I threw a punch at one of 'em.
I didn't hit him hard,

but that sealed my doom.
They took me to a room
and they locked the door behind me
and there was four guys, four cops there
kicking me in the head.
As a result of the kicks in the head they fractured my
    eardrum,
and, uh,
I couldn't hear
on both ears.
I was deaf,
worse than I am now.
(He pulls out one of his hearing aids)
So
from that day on
I, I had a hate in me,
even now.
I don't like to hate, never do,
the way that my Uncle Abraham told me that to hate is to
    waste
energy and you mess with man upstairs,
but I had an insane hatred
for white policemen.
I used to read the paper—it's awful, it's awful—
if I would read about a cop shot down in the street,
killed,
dead,
a human being!
a fellow human being?
I say,
"So, you know, you know, so what,

maybe he's one of those motherfuckers that,
y'know . . ."
and I still get things like that.
I know this society.
I'm hooked on the news at six and the newspapers
and every morning I read injustices
and poor Margaret has to put up with me
'cause I rave and I rant and I walk around here.
I gotta eat breakfast over there,
I can't eat breakfast with her
'cause I tell her,
"These goddamned peckerwoods,"
so she puts me out there.
But I don't hate rednecks and peckerwoods,
and when I moved in here
it's all peckerwoods.
I had to put out my big Mexican flag out of my van.
Oh heck,
I told my kids a long time ago, fears that I had—
not physically inferior,
I grew up with the idea that
whites are
physically . . .
I still got that—see, that's a prejudice,
that whites are physically afraid of, of
minorities,
people of color, Blacks and Mexicans.
It's a physical thing,
it's a mental, mental thing that they're physically afraid.
I, I can still see it,
I can still see it,

and, and,
and, uh-uh,
I love to see it.
It's just how I am.
I can't help myself when I see
the right
person
do the right thing,
if I see the right white guy
or the right
Mexican walk down the mall
(*He makes a face and laughs*)
and the whites,
you know, they go into their thing already.
I don't like to see a gang of *cholos*
walking around,
you know, threatening people
with their ugly faces—
that's something else.
Well, they put on the mask—you ever notice that?—
it's sort of a mask,
it's, uh . . .
(*He stands up and mimics them*)
You know how they stand in your face with the ugly faces.
Damn, man,
I'd like to kill their dads.
That's what I always think about.
I always dream of that—
break into their houses and drag their dads out.
Well, you see, that relieves me.
But, you see, I still have that prejudice against whites.

I'm not a racist!
But I have white friends, though,
but I don't even see them as whites!
I don't even see them as whites! And my boys,
I had a lot of anxiety, I told
them, "Cooperate, man,
something happens,
your hands . . .
(Puts his hands up)
let them call you what they want,
be sure tell me who they are."
But they never told me.
Stephen was in Stanford!
Came home one weekend
to sing
with the band.
One night
cop pulled a gun at his head.
It drove me crazy—
it's still going on,
it's still going on.
How you think
a
father feels,
stuff that happened to me
fifty years
ago
happened to my son?
Man!
They didn't tell me right away,
because it would make me sick,

it would make me sick,
and, uh,
my oldest son, Rudy.
Didn't they,
Margaret,
insult him one time and they pulled you over . . .
the Alhambra cops, they pulled you over
and, aww, man . . .
My enemy.

The Territory

These Curious People

Stanley K. Sheinbaum Former president, Los Angeles Police Commission

(A beautiful house in Brentwood. There is art on all the walls. The art has a real spirit to it. These are the paintings by his wife, Betty Sheinbaum. There is a large living room, an office off the living room which you can see. It is mostly made of wood, lots of papers and books. The office of a writer. There are glass windows that look out on a pool, a garden, a view. Behind us is a kitchen where his wife, Betty, was, but eventually she leaves. Stanley is sitting at a round wooden table with a cup of coffee. He is in a striped shirt and khaki pants and loafers. He has a beard. He is tall, and about seventy-three years old. He seems gruff, but when he smiles or laughs, his face lights up the room. It's very unusual. He has the smile and laugh of a highly spiritual, joyous, old woman, like a grandmother who has really been around. There is a bird inside the house which occasionally chirps.)

V ery
interesting thing happened.
Like a week and a half *(very thoughtfully trying to
    remember),*
Maxine Waters calls me up—
You know who she is?
We're very good friends—
she calls me up and she says,
"Ya gotta come with me.
I been going down to Nickerson Gardens
and

the cops come in and break up these gang meetings
and these are gang meetings
for the purpose of truces."
(I was momentarily distracted)
Pay attention.
The next Saturday afternoon,
the next day even,
I go down with her,
uh,
to,
uh,
Nickerson Gardens
(an abrupt stop, and
second pause, as if he's forgotten something for a moment)
and I see a whole bunch of, uh,
police car
sirens and the lights
and I say, "What the hell's going on here?"
So sure enough, I pull in there
(three-second pause).
We pull in there
and, uh,
I ask a cop what's going on
and he says,
"Well, we got a call for help."
There's a gang meeting over there.
There's a community park there and there's a gym
and I go down to the . . .
we go down to the gang meeting
and half of 'em
outside of the

gym
and half of 'em
inside
and here's about a hundred cops lined up over here
and about another hundred
over here
and, uh,
I go
into the, uh,
into the group of gang members who were outside.
Even Maxine got scared by this.
I gotta tell you I was brought up in Harlem.
I just have a feel for what I can do and what I can't do
and I did that.
And I spent about
two, two
hours talkin' to these guys.
Some of these guys were ready to kill me.
(A bird chirps loudly; maybe this is a parakeet or an inside
bird)
I'm the police commissioner
and therefore a cop
and therefore all the things that went along with being a
    cop.
It was a very interesting experience, God knows.
One guy who was really disheveled and disjointed
and disfigured
opens up his whole body
and it's clear he's been shot across . . .
not in that . . . not in that day,
months or years before,

and, you know,
these guys have been through the wars down there
and,
you know, I hung around long enough that I could talk to
    them,
get some insights.
But the cops were mad,
they were really mad
that I would go talk to them
and not talk to them
and I knew that if I went and talked to them
I'd have bigger problems here
But I also knew as I was doing this,
I knew they were gonna be pissed.
Two days I got a letter
and I was . . .
the letter really pleased me in some way.
It was very respectful.
"You went in and talked to our enemy."
Gangs are their enemy.
And so
I marched down to Seventy-seventh
and, uh,
I said, "Fuck you,
I can come in here
anytime I want and talk to you."
Yeah, at roll call.
I said, uh,
"This is a shot I had at talking to these
curious people
about whom I know nothing

and I wanna learn.
Don't you want me to learn about 'em?"
You know, that kind of thing.
At the same time, I had been on this kick,
as I told you before, of . . .
of fighting for what's right for the cops,
because they haven't gotten what they should.
I mean, this city has abused both sides.
The city has abused the cops.
Don't ever forget that.
If you want me to give you an hour on that, I'll give you an
    hour on
that.
Uh,
and at the end,
uh,
I knew I hadn't won when they said,
"So which side are you on?"
When I said, I said, it's . . .
my answer was
"Why do I have to be on a side?"
Yu, yuh, yeh know.
Why do I have to be on a side?
There's a problem here.

When I Finally Got My Vision/Nightclothes

Michael Zinzun Representative, Coalition Against Police Abuse

(In his office at Coalition Against Police Abuse. There are very bloody and disturbing photographs of victims of police abuse. The most disturbing one was a man with part of his skull blown off and part of his body in the chest area blown off, so that you can see the organs. There is a large white banner with a black circle and a panther. The black panther is the image from the Black Panther Party. Above the circle is "All Power to the People." At the bottom is "Support Our Youth, Support the Truce.")

I witnessed police abuse.
It was
about one o'clock in the morning
and, um,
I was asleep,
like
so many of the other neighbors,
and I hear this guy calling out for help.
So myself and other people came out in socks
and gowns
and, you know,
nightclothes
and we came out so quickly we saw the police had this
     brother
handcuffed
and they was beatin' the shit out of him!

You see,
Eugene Rivers was his name
and, uh,
we had our community center here
and they was doin' it right across the street from it.
So I went out there 'long with other people and we
    demanded they stop.
They tried to hide him by draggin' him away and we
    followed him
and told him they gonna stop.
They singled me out.
They began Macing the crowd, sayin' it was hostile.
They began
shootin' the Mace to get everybody back.
They singled me out.
I was handcuffed.
Um,
when I got Maced I moved back
but as I was goin' back I didn't go back to the center,
I ended up goin' around this . . .
it was a darkened
unlit area.
And when I finally got my vision
I said I ain't goin' this way with them police behind me,
so I turned back around, and when I did,
they Maced me again
and I went down on one knee
and all I could do was feel all these police stompin' on my
    back.
(He is smiling)
And I was thinkin' . . . I said

why, sure am glad they got them soft walkin' shoes on,
because when the patrolmen, you know, they have them
cushions,
so every stomp,
it wasn't a direct hard old . . .
yeah
type thing.
So
then they handcuffed me.
I said they . . .
well,
I can take this,
we'll deal with this tamarr [sic],
and they handcuffed me.
And then one of them lifted my
head up—
I was on my stomach—
he lifted me from behind
and hit me with a billy club
and struck me in the
side of the head,
which give me about forty stitches—
the straight billy club,
it wasn't a
P-28, the one with the side handle.
Now, I thought in my mind, said hunh,
they couldn't even knock me out,
they in trouble now.
You see what I'm sayin'?
'Cause I knew what we were gonna do,
'cause I dealt with police abuse

and I knew how to organize.
I say they couldn't even knock me out,
and so as I was layin' there
they was all standin' around me.
They still was Macing, the crowd was gettin' larger and
     larger and
larger
and more police was comin'.
One these pigs stepped outta the crowd with his flashlight,
caught me right in my eye,
and you can still see the stitches *(He lowers his lid and*
     shows it)
and
exploded the optic nerve to the brain,
ya see,
and boom *(He snaps his fingers)*
that was it.
I couldn't see no more since then.
I mean, they . . .
they took me to the hospital
and the doctor said, "Well, we can sew this eyelid up and
     these
stitches here
but
I don't think we can do nothin' for that eye."
So when I got out I got a CAT scan,
you know,
and
they said,
"It's gone."
So I still didn't understand it but I said

well,
I'm just gonna keep strugglin'.
We mobilized
to the point where we were able
to get two officers fired,
two officers had to go to trial,
and
the city on an eye
had to cough up one point two million dollars
and so
that's why
I am able to be here every day,
because that money's bein' used to further the struggle.
I ain't got no big Cadillac,
I ain't got no gold . . .
I ain't got no
expensive shoes or clothes.
What we do have
is an opportunity to keep struggling and to do research and to
organize.

They

Jason Sanford Actor

(A rainstorm in February 1993. Saturday afternoon.
We are in an office at the Mark Taper Forum. Lamplight. A handsome white man in his late twenties
wearing blue jeans and a plaid shirt and Timber-
land boots. He played tennis in competition for
years and looks like a tennis player.)

Who's they?
That's interesting,
'cause the they is
a combination of a lot of things.
Being brought up in Santa Barbara,
it's a little bit different saying "they" than being brought up in,
um,
LA,
I think,
'cause
being brought up in Santa Barbara
you don't see a lot of blacks.
You see Mexicans,
you see some Chinese,
but you don't see blacks.
There was maybe two black people in my school.
I don't know, you don't say
black
or you don't say
Negro
or,

no,
yeah,
you really don't.
I work with one.
Um,
because
of what I look like
I don't know if I'd been beaten.
I sure the hell would have been arrested
and pushed down on the ground.
I don't think it would have gone as far.
It wouldn't have.
Even the times that I have been arrested
they always make comments
about God, you look like Mr.,
uh,
all-American white boy.
That has actually been said to me
by a . . . by a
cop.
Ya know,
"Why do you have so many warrants?"
Ya know . . .
"Shouldn't you be takin' care of this?"
Ya know . . .
"You look like an all-American white boy.
You look responsible."
And
I remember being arrested in Santa Barbara one time
and
driving back

in the cop car
and having a conversation about tennis
with the cops.
So,
ah,
I'm sure I'm seen by the police totally different
than a black man.

Broad Daylight
Anonymous Young Man
Former gang member

(Saturday, fall, sunny. He is wearing black pants
and an oversized tee shirt. He is living with his
mother after having recently gotten out of jail. His
mother lives in a fancy apartment building, with
pool, recreation room, etc. We are in one of the
lounges. He has a goatee and wears his hair
pulled back in a ponytail. He is black but looks
Latino.)

They kind of respected their elders,
as far as,
not robbing them,
but then a lot of . . .
as I got older I noticed,
like the younger ones,
the lot of the
respect,
it
just like
disappeared,
'cause I . . . when I was younger it was like
if the police had
me and a couple other guys in the middle of the street
on our knees,
the older people would
come out and question.
They like . . .
"Take 'em to jail,"

because of that loss of respect,
you know,
of the elders
by the younger ones,
losing the respect of the elders.
When I went to the Valley
I felt more respect,
because when
I was in the
Valley
I was right there with rivals.
It's like I could walk right over
and it was rivals
and the way I felt was like
strong,
'cause when I moved out there
I didn't bring
all my homeboys
with me
and it's like I used to tell them,
my rivals,
I used to tell 'em, "Man,
I'm a one-man army."
I would joke about it.
I say,
"I don't need my homeboys
and everything."
Me and my brother,
we used to call ourselves the Blues Brothers,
because it was two of us
and we

would go and we either have our blue rags hanging and go
    right up
there in their neighborhood where there are
Bloods
and go right up in the apartments
and there could be a crowd of 'em
and we would pass by—
"What's up, cuz?"—
and keep goin'
and every now and then
they might say
something
but the majority of 'em
knew that I keep a gun on me
and every now and then
there would be broad daylight like this.
Some of 'em
would try and test me and say,
"well, he ain't fixin' ta shoot me in this broad daylight,"
you know,
and then
when they do
then you know
I either end up chasin' 'em,
shootin' at 'em or shootin'
whatever.
'Cause they thought ain't nobody that stupid
to shoot people in broad daylight.
And I was the opposite.
My theory was when you shoot somebody in broad daylight
people gonna be mostly scared,

they not gonna just sit there and look at you,
you know, to identify you.
I figure there's gonna be like
"I gotta run"
and I figure they just gonna be too scared to see who you
    are to
identify you.
That's where the reputation
came,
'cause they didn't know when I was comin',
broad daylight
or at night.
My favorite song?
I like oldies.
My favorite song is by Atlantic Star.
It's called
"Am I Dreamin'?"

Surfer's Desert

Mike Davis LA-based writer and urban critic

(Sunday, May 1993. The day after the verdict in the second federal trial against Koon, Powell, Wind, Briseno. The entire city is sighing in relief. He is less impressed with it all, and said he thought it was all a hoax. He is wearing a red shirt. He is of Irish descent. Looks kind of like Robert Redford. Prematurely white hair, light eyes. He is with his daughter, who is about nine years old and is visiting him from Ireland. She is very disciplined. We are having lunch in a restaurant in the Biltmore Hotel in downtown Los Angeles. Opulent. He is eating a hamburger and drinking coffee.)

But I mean . . .
For all the talk about the civil rights movement, I mean, we
    need it
today like we need sunshine
and, and, and, and fresh air, because
the price of it is the self-destruction
of a generation of kids who are
so hip and so smart
but who in some way,
so susceptible to despair across, you know, across
the board.
And the other thing that nobody's talking about
in the city is the gang
truce has been something of a miracle, you know.
It's the sign of
a generation

that won't commit suicide.
It's
it's a reestablishment of contact with . . .
with traditions, you know,
you know of
you know of pride and struggle.
But at the same time, on the East Side we have the *worst*
    Latino gang
war in history.
One weekend, we have seventeen, um, Latino kids killed in
    gang-related
stuff.
New immigrants' kids, who couple of years ago wouldn't be
    in gangs
at all, are now joining in in large numbers.
And nobody's kind of gettin' up and sayin', "Look, this is an
emergency.
Let's put the resources out to at least reestablish
contact with,
with, with the kids."
The fear in this city of talking to gang members,
talking to kids.
In the last instance, if you peel away words like, you
know, "gang-banger" and "looter" and stuff,
this is a city at war with
its own children,
and it refuses to talk to those children,
And the city doesn't want to face these kids,
or talk to its kids,
And I think,
I think it's the same thing probably with the white

middle class,
but I guess for me to sound like a bit of a sop,
for I've come to realize what we've lost.
'Cause everything I've come to like about Southern
    California growing
up here as, as, as a kid.
It's when I joined the civil rights movement in the early
    sixties.
I mean, the vision was like,
yeah, I mean what the civil rights movement was about . . .
is that black kids can be surfers too.
I mean, there were a core of freedoms
and opportunities and pleasures that have been established,
again like, you know,
working-class white kids in my generation.
My parents hitchhiked out here from Ohio.
You know, I grew up with, with, with,
you know, Okies and Dust Bowl refugees
and we got free junior college education.
There were plenty—
there were more jobs than
you could imagine out there.
We could go to the beach,
we could race our cars.
I'm not saying that, you know, it was utopia or
happiness
but it was . . .
it was something incredibly important.
And the whole ethos of the civil rights struggle and
    movement for
equality in California's history

was to make this available to everyone.
The irony now is that even white privileged kids
are losing these things.
I mean, there *is* no freedom of movement or right of
    assembly for
youth.
I mean,
the only permitted legal activity anymore
is, is being in a mall shopping.
I mean, cruising has been
totally eliminated because it's . . .
it leads to gang warfare or some other crazy notion.
The beaches are patrolled by helicopters
and, and police dune buggies.
It's illegal to sleep on the, the beach anymore.
So the very things that are defined, you know, our kind of
    populace,
Southern California, kind of working-class Southern
    California,
have been destroyed.
People go to the desert to live in armed compounds
and to tear up the Joshua trees
instead of to, you know, to find
the freedom that you used to be able to find
in, in, you know,
the desert.

Lightning But No Rain

Theresa Allison Founder of
Mothers Reclaiming Our Children (Mothers
ROC) Mother of gang truce architect Dewayne
Holmes

(Amazing black hat and bracelets on both arms.
Beautiful rings.)

Mothers ROC came about right after my nephew was
   killed,
November the 29th of '91.
After the death of my nephew, my son
Dewayne
thought about a peace among,
you know, the, the guys in the project—
I don't want to say gangs—
the young men.
The truce, they started meeting every Sunday,
so I thought about
a group of mothers gettin' together,
so I thought about
the words
Reclaiming Our Children.
I knew that there was
a lot of kids going to prison,
a lot of kids going to the cemetery
by the hands of our enemy,
the unjust system.
Then my son Dewayne was sentenced for a crime he did
   not do.

When they killed Tiny—
when I say "they," I mean the police.
They shot forty-three times.
Five bullets went into Tiny.
No bullets went in nobody else's body.
I think what they do, they want to make it look like a
    drive-by
shooting.
See, when the gangs
shoot at each other,
it's a lot of 'em
fire
(*She shows the shooting with her hand*)
bullets.
When they killed Tiny, they were in unmarked cars.
When they shot my nephew, they were dressed like gang
    members,
duck-walkin',
with hard beanies, jackets, no badges or anything,
all over the project,
like
birds!
This was going to be listed as a drive-by shooting,
and then they were gonna put
it on another project.
This is what they do all the time.
And for some reason the lights was out in the project,
'cause Tiny was goin' around
gatherin' up the children,
'cause when the lights go out in the projects,
there's a lot of shooting.

So when I left the Fox Hill Mall
I felt something was wrong,
but I didn't think it was my family,
'cause that day look like the crucifixion of Jesus.
I told people, "Doesn't this look like
the crucifixion of Jesus?" and they say,
"You right."
It was the weirdest time of my life,
it was the weirdest feeling.
It was lightning,
no rain!
And when I got back home my daughter was runnin' down
    La Brea
wid her two little girls and she was cryin'.
My daughter told me then
that Tiny,
that Tiny had been killed.
The day we had Tiny's funeral
it was so many people,
and me
being a strong Catholic,
it reminded me of the time
that Jesus took that one loaf of bread and made a whole,
it was just like that.
All of Tiny's death told me
that
a change must come,
really
a change got to come.
My son changed.
(She's crying)

Other guys in Watts changed.
Our life totally changed
from happy people
to hurting people.
I mean hurting people,
I mean *hurting,*
pain.
When we came back from the funeral,
we had a demonstration,
so I had a
great coalition.
I mean, I,
I mean it was . . .
I'm tellin' ya,
I'm tellin' you eight hundred fifty people,
nothin' but Spanish people,
that caravan,
I had white folks!
That in itself . . .
They don't want,
they don't want the peace,
they don't want us comin' together.
So after that they wanted my son more.
They wanted Dewayne more.
So when they attack my son,
again the lights was out in the project for some reason.
He was walkin' slow.
They told him
to give him his driver's license,
but they kept insisting he was another person,
Damian Holmes,

or some other Holmes they use,
other than Dewayne Holmes.
So they had him in a car.
So some people ran and got me.
We surrounded the police car,
we gonna turn it over,
we gonna turn it over.
Some laid on the ground.
I laid at the front part of the bumper, and one little girl—
    she was
about eighteen but she looked like twelve—
she was underneath the back wheel, so they couldn't
    roll.
If they rolled, they would have hit somebody,
people were all over the ground.
I told him, I said, "My son don't have a
warrant."
He said, "Oh yes he does."
I said, "Okay, run his name through this computer."
"Oh, we can't do that."
I said, "You a lie.
You do it anytime you want to arrest them."
So they kept saying they couldn't use it, they had to take
    him to the
station,
to run his name.
"But maybe he doesn't have anything."
"We just have to take him to the station."
Now, you
know and I know too,
before the police stop you for a traffic ticket

they done ran your license plate.
I mean, they know who you are,
you know.
They knew he was,
they knew he was Dewayne Holmes,
they knew he was Sniper!
I said, "Look, I'm not gonna move.
You not gonna kill my son like you killed my nephew."
So the police happened to pull the car up a little bit and hit
    my leg.
Dewayne said, "Don't you hit my mother!"
But we, I already told him, "We gonna turn the car over,
    Dewayne,
we gonna turn it over."
They were not gonna kill my son.
And that was their intention, to kill my son,
they still wanna kill my son,
they do! *(She cries)*
So then
the sergeant came
and he told the man,
he said, "It's not your son.
I made a mistake."
Somebody yell outta the car,
"Make 'em tell him they're sorry."
So the cop had to say,
"I'm sorry,"
that they didn't want to have . . .
After that Dewayne couldn't walk,
go from one side of the project to another.
They was trying to get my son,

to stop us, to stop
the demonstration,
to stop
us from protestin' against them,
to stop the world from knowing
that they corrupt.
LA supposed to be the best police officers in the world,
and if everybody all over the world knows
they the corrupt one,
then
that's the problem,
they been doin' it.
They used to take our kids
from one project
and drop 'em into another gang
zone and leave 'em in there
and let those guys kill 'em
and then say it's a gang-related thing,
hear me?
They picked my son up several times
and dropped him in another project
when he was just a little boy.
They've done it to my kid,
they'll do it to your kid.
It's the color, because we're Black.
The woman that killed Tiny,
she had a big
plaque—woman of the year!
Yeah, she shot him in the face,
her and her partner, we call 'em Cagney and Lacey,
and she is . . .

a little—
I can't give you the name—
how she use to go in an' pull these kids,
I mean from twelve years old,
and kick 'em and hit their heads against trees
and stomp on the ground.
Why you got to do Black kids like that?
Why couldn't you handcuff 'em and take 'em to jail?
Why couldn't they handcuff my nephew Tiny
and just take him to jail?
After they done shot him down,
he couldn't move! *(she cries)*
Why they have to shoot him in the face?
Doesn't seem like they killin' him
to keep from him sayin' what they said to him.
(Crying and an abrupt change)
They coverin' up!
'Cause they know they killed him wrong!
I'm not sayin' they were just gunnin' for Tiny,
but they not men enough,
they not men or women enough to say, "Hey, I killed the
    wrong person."
These police officers are just like you and I.
Take that damn uniform off of 'em,
they the same as you and I.
Why do they have so much power?
Why does the system work for them?
Where can we go
to get the justice that they have?
Ts tuh!
Where? *(crying)*

Then they took my child!
I was tired.
I have heart problems.
I went away
and they took him while I was gone.

A Bloodstained Banner

Cornel West Scholar

(He is in a three-piece navy-blue suit with a pocket
watch and he has on cuff links. Eyeglasses. Books
everywhere, papers on the desk. It is as if the desk,
which is two-sided, is a fortress. The answering
machine clicks and there are two beeps.)

You sell
at the
most profitable price
and it's inescapable, it's ubiquitous,
you're selling things,
you're selling things at the most profitable price
and you're trying to gain
access
to power and property
and pleasure
by any means you cayan,
you see,
and thal [sic] are two different things.
On the one hand
there's
like duh frontier myth in America,
right? *(barely audible on the word "right")*
That we *(hard to hear that "we")* gain some moral and
    plitical [sic]
regeneration
and expansion by means of conquest and dispossession of
    duh

people's land.
So I mean a, uh,
Richard Slotkin talks about dis in terms
of being a gunfighterr *(grabbing the "r")* nation.
If in fact our major myth is that of the fron*teer*,
the way in which you expand the fron*teer*
(He is leaning forward, with his head down close to the desk, his
glasses seeming to sit on top of his ears, and screwing up his face, as
he literally puts his body into the idea)
is by being a gunfighter.
So many *he*roes,
these *cow*boys
wit dere gu-uns
Now, you can imagine
on *one* level
dat's done
because you wanna
expand
possibilities for the market,
extract resources from the land,
even as you subordinate the peoples who are on that land.
Well, on another level
it's a deep machismo
ethic,
which is
gangsterous,
eh? *(almost as if he's saying "okay?" or "right?")*
That to be a
mayan

who engages in this
means ta put othuhs down,
ta be *tough*, ta be cold
and meanspirited, and so forth.
To be like Rambo,
as this brother Stallone made big money in the last decade,
right?
Uh, and
this kinda gangsterous orientation,
which as we know,
ya know,
has a long history in black *and* white,
uh, and
in rap music these days—
you know, gangster rap,
which is deeply resistant of, uh, against *racism* and so forth
but so centered on machismo identity because
you *tough*
like a soldier,
you like a, uh, military mayan,
you, you can best,
you're better *thayan,* uh, these other
military men that you're fightin', against,
you can outpolice the police,
you can outbrutalize the police brutality,
the police who are being brutal and so forth
and so on.
So you're playing exactly the same game, as it were,
and racial *reasoning,* I think, oftentimes has been construed
     as an
attempt of black people

all coming together
in order to
both protect
each other
but usually the men
who will serve as the policing agents,
therefore the interests of black *women*
are subordinated
and the black men
become the
machismo heroes,
because they're the ones who defy
and women can't do that.
Why,
because,
you know, these folks who you're defying
themselves are machismo,
so you need a machismo person to respond to the
    machismo.
So you get dis
encounter
between two machismo heroes,
you see,
and it takes courage.
I don't wanna downplay these machismo heroes
but it's still within a patriarchal mode,
it's still very much within a patriarchal mode,
and it reproduces and recycles the same kinda conception of
    what it
is to engage
in

struggle
and what it is to
attempt to gain
some progress,
as it were,
and hence what I think we end up with is a certain kind
of *turf* policing.
The best we can do
is hold up
a bloodstained banner
of a black struggle that is rooted in moral vision
and yet
acknowledging the fact
that a power struggle
will be fundamental for any change, so you don't wanna be
      naive
and on the other hand you don't also wanna just become
amoral at the same time
or give up
on
the broader possibilities of hu*mann*
beings engaging in interaction that accents our
      humanness,
more than simply our, uh,
our delusory foundations,
race or gender or whatever.
Uh,
but!
ass,
you know,
ass the bess we can do,

ass the bess anybody can do at any moment of human
    history
is simply hold up the bess of what you see in the pass,
no guarantee whatso*ever*
that, one, it will ever triumph or, *two*,
that it will ever gain a mass following.
I mean for *me*
it, it, it,
the real marking was the, uh,
the demise of
the innernat . . .
the demise of
the Black Panther Party, which was the
last representation
of
inter*nat*ionalism
and multi*racial*ism
grounded in the black community,
you see,
'cause
what the Black Panther Party was trying to do
was ta take duh best of the boldness and defiance of
    Malcolm X,
which is often machismo-driven
but also quite authentic
in terms of its critiques of white supremacy, but also
link it to
a certain internationalism
that acknowledged the roles of people of color,
that acknowledged the role of progressive white persons,
that acknowledged the role of all

whosoever will
identify
with poor
people and working people,
and, uh,
Huey Newton and Bobby Seale, given all their faults,
did have that kind of broad,
all-embracing vision that people forget.
I mean that broad international perspective, you see,
and it was not closing ranks,
it was not just a kind of narrow black nationalism that they
    were
putting forward,
at all,
at all.
Uh,
but once that went under
it became very clear
that we were in a moment of dissarray,
and, of course,
the conservative forces,
business classes, especially corporate elites, unified,
    consolidated, and
then
were able to bring to bear their own policies
in reshaping society,
primarily in their own interest,
and that's what we been up against for the past nineteen,
    twenty
years.
Yeah.

No, well, good luck,
good luck
indeed in deed.
I'm always pullin' an' prayin' for ya.

(BLACKOUT)

Here's a Nobody

Carmen

Angela King Aunt of Rodney King

A shop in Pasadena. A very, very rainy day. We are sitting in the back of the shop. She insists that my assistant, Kishisha Jefferson, join us, because she thought it was not good to make Kishisha sit in the car in the rain. We are in the back of her shop. There are work tables with paints, etc. She makes T-shirts. The shop itself is a boutique with clothing for men, women, and children. Some of the clothing is Afrocentric in design, other items are more mainstream. She is a powerful looking woman with a direct gaze and wavy hair, and a warmth that is natural, even when it is not intended. She looks as though she has Native American ancestry. She is wearing a white sweater, a long skirt, and boots. She smokes a cigarette. There is an iron gate at the main door that is painted white. There is a small television in the back where we are. She lives in an area behind where we are sitting. The interview was actually scheduled for the day before, but she was reluctant to speak with me, because when I arrived Kishisha was in the car. (Kishisha normally drove me to, but did not attend, each interview.) It is ironic that now at the rescheduled time, she insists that Kishisha join us.

Our life is something like,
uh,
what's the name of that picture
with Dorothy Dandridge
when she was like
a prostitute and the guy she met was in the Air Force—
the service?
Carmen.

Dorothy Dandridge
and Harry Belafonte—
that was us.
How they partied a lot,
and the guy in in the Air Force,
the way he was conservative,
was my father.
We were brought up
for about five or six years like that.
The part where she was . . .
she got in some trouble,
the way my mom,
she cut my father:
They were at the NCO club,
they got to drinkin',
and they went to jail out on the base.
She stabbed him—
oh yeah, honey—
he had a scar on his neck.
She went to jail behind that.
We were twelve or thirteen years old.
It seems like it should have been in a movie:
separated and
livin' in different homes
and then joinin' back together in different homes
and reuniting.
My brother and I were only two that stayed together,
and that brother was the father of Rodney.
Things that we did
like goin fishin',
and then on Franklin,

the Sacramento River,
and then . . .
I ain't never seen nothing like it in my life.
It was me, Rodney, Paul, and Sam,
Rodney's friend,
and I looked up and Rodney was down in the water—
had his pants rolled,
feet and all,
like these Africans—
done caught him a big old
trout
by his—
with his hands.
That was the worst mess I seen.
Got him like this here:
"I got him, I got him!
I got a big . . .
'bout that big . . ."
I said, "Boy, you sure you ain't got some African in you?"
Ooh,
yeah,
I'm talkin 'bout them wild Africans,
not one them well raised ones.
Like with a fish hook?
But to see somebody down in the water with the pants
      rolled up
like this here . . .
I said "Get out of there you scaring 'em, you scaring um!"
"Naw, I got this one, I got this one!"
And comin' up there with this big old trout.
Hand fishin'!

He was the only one I saw down in there in that water,
him and this other guy, this big Mexican guy,
Sam?
And he's the only one I seen catch fish like that.
The rest of 'em got poles.
Down in there with them pants up like that.
That remind me of what I see in Africa somewhere.
I ain't never seen nobody fish with their hands.
Talkin' bout "I ain't got time to wait."
That's why I call him greedy.
I'm 'a ask him does he remember that.
He oughta remember it, he was bout sixteen or seventeen
    years old.
Um, Um, Um . . .
He—Glen,
Rodney—
went through three plastic surgeons
just to look like Rodney again.
Galen called to say cops done beat Glen up, talkin about
    Rodney,
I said "What?"
And when I was just turning the channels,
I saw this white car . . .
And he looked just like his father.
I don't know if it's when you lose a life
it comes back in somebody else.
Oh, you should have seen him.
It's a hell of a look.
I, I mean you wouldn't have known him
to look at him now.
I tell him he's got a lot to be thankful for—
a hell of a lot:

He couldn't talk,
just, "Der, der, der."
I said, Goddamn!
I was right here
when it happened.
You want me to tell it?
Ah . . .
(She starts crying;
she makes about seven sobs)
Oh, man.
It just came out.
(She gets up and goes away to the door. The hammering is
louder. There are two hammers, in different places, as if
above or next door. The hammers really sound like a
dialogue, and there are cars outside, and rain. The dripping
is very close.)
Ah.
It comes up every now and then.
Don't worry.
Just burst out . . .
Um . . .
I told you this whole thing is too much.
It's hurting an' then you're happy,
'specially when I get to thinking about such treacherous
  people out there.
We weren't raised like this.
We weren't raised with no black and white thing.
We were raised with all kinds of friends:
Mexicans, Indians, Blacks, Whites, Chinese.
You never would have known that something like this would
  happen to us.
And now it's such a shock.

And then the media,
and then, uh,
"What the hell did you get on there tellin' them people?"
I said,
"Leave me the hell alone,"—
this is the other end of the family—
"them people wants to know.
I'm not gonna keep my doors closed up."
I'm arguin' with them.
"Well tell them this here,
and the next time you get on there,
you tell these people this"
I'm not tellin' these people a damn thing—
all this here went through my damn mind.
I get up here,
"Well Mrs. King so and so and so and so."
Um hum, yeah.
And then they . . .
You know I get up here,
"Oh should I say this should I say that?"
Just a mess, the whole thing.
The media came to me 'cause I was a relative
of Rodney's
and his mother
Dessa wasn't gonna talk—
they didn't because of they religion,
they didn't want to get involved in a political . . .
whatever this thing was.
But I didn't give a damn if it was the president's . . .
whatever it was,
my brother's son out there was lookin' like hell,

that I saw in that bed, and I was gonna fight for every bit of
our justice
and fairness.
I didn't care nothin' 'bout no religious . . .
You know, the President,
he's the top thing,
you know, they cared about him;
that's the way I cared about Glen,
you know, Rodney.
That's the way I feel,
you know, a higher sorts.
It could have been my mother.
But I'm not gonna say that.
You see how everybody rave when something happens with
 the
President of the United States?
Okay, here's a nobody,
but the way they beat him,
this is the way I felt towards him.
You understand what I'm sayin' now?
You do? *(really making sure that I mean what I say)*
Alright.
(a breath, and more speed as she proceeds)
That's the way I felt.
I didn't give a damn about no religious
nothin' else,
I wanted justice,
and I wanted whatever
them things had comin' to them done to them,
regardless—you can call it revenge or whatever, but
what I saw on that video,

on that TV,
that was a
mess.
And I just heard him holler,
that's what got me 'while ago.
And then they say,
"Motorist."
And then I look and saw that white car,
and then I saw him out on that ground,
I heard him hollerin',
I recognized him
out on that ground.
Um . . .
Um . . .
That Koon—
that's the one in that whole trial—
that man showed no kind of remorse at all,
you know that?
He sit there like, "It ain't no big thing,
and I
will do it again."
That's the way he looked.
You ever seen him?
And he smile at you.
I don't know how,
I don't *even* know how . . .
the nerve,
the audacity.
And even Briseno,
he's gonna get on there . . .
that's what I'm tellin'

Rodney:
"They tryin'
to do everything they possibly can—*anything* they can—
to make you look bad to the people.
Because of what they had,
that, you know,
what's been done to them—
they've been embarrassed,
and they caught them,
you know, on video,
beatin' you like that,
and the public saw it,
they tryin' to do anything they can to discredit you.
You need to get somewhere and sit down."
I didn't hear nobody mention
about 'em having a bug.
It was like a screw
about the size of my thumb
on the bumper—
on the Blazer—
and they were trailin' him everywhere he went.
This is how they knew
where he was goin',
or how
every time you turn around Rodney King's encounter with
  the law
they had a *screw*.
This is how they had him tagged down.
Uhm hum. Uhm hum.
Right after that Hollywood incident
with that prostitute

and on the phone,
I can hear the echo.
And when I hang up someone is still there.
And then most of the time
I be talkin' crazy anyway
so it doesn't matter.
And why? I have no idea.
But they say there's nothing they can do about the taps.
I've called the telephone company
but
something—it being interfered with the federal government,
so it wasn't nothin' they could do about it.
But I know one thing:
Half the things I said to them on there—
it's been goin' on for a while—
I drop through profanity,
I do,
'cause I get on there, I be wantin' to talk and relax, you
  know,
and here something click up and click up
and that's when I get started.
I do.
'Cause you have to stop and catch yourself,
you can't just talk comfortable.
Yeah.

Where the Water Is
Sergeant Charles Duke
Special Weapons and Tactics Unit, LAPD Use-of-force expert for the defense witness, Simi Valley and Federal trials

(He is standing with a baton. He is wearing glasses and a uniform and black shoes.)

Powell holds the baton
like this
and that is
not a good . . .
the proper way of holding the baton
is like this.
So one of the things
they keep talking about
why did it take fifty-six baton blows.
Powell has no strength and no power
in his baton strikes.
The whole thing boils down to . . .
Powell was ineffective with the baton.
You're aware
that that night
he went to baton training
and the sergeant held him afterward
because he was weak and inefficient with the baton
    training.
That night. That night.
He should have been taken out of the field.

He needed to be taken up to the academy and had a couple days of
instruction get him back into
focus.
(*He drinks water*)
Oh, I know what I was gonna do.
Prior to this
we lost upper-body-control holds,
in 1982.
If we had upper-body-control holds
involved in this,
this tape woulda never been on,
this incident woulda lasted about
fifteen seconds.
The reason that we lost upper-body-control holds . . .
because we had something like
seventeen to twenty deaths in a period of about 1975–76 to
1982, and
they said it was associated with its being used on Blacks
and Blacks were dying.
Now,
the so-called community leaders
came forward and complained
(*He drinks water*)
and they started a hysteria
about the upper-body-control holds—
that it was inhumane use of force—
so it got elevated from intermediate use of force,
which is the same category as a baton,
to deadly force,
and what I told you was that it was used

in all but one of the incidents.
High levels of PCP and cocaine were found in the systems
of those people it was used on.
If PCP and cocaine did not correlate into the equation
of why people were dying,
how come we used it since the fifties
and we had maybe in a ten-year period one incident of a
    death?
The use of force policy hasn't changed since this incident.
And Gilbert Lindsay,
who was a really neat man,
when he saw a demonstration with the baton
he made a statement
that "you're not gonna beat my people with the baton,
I want you to use the chokehold on 'em."
And a couple other people said,
"I don't care you beat em into submission,
you break their bones,
you're not chokin' 'em anymore."
So the political framework was laid
for eliminating upper-body-control holds,
and Daryl Gates—
I believe, but I can't prove it—
but his attitude supports it.
He
and his command staff
and I started
use-of-force reports come through my office,
so I review 'em and I look for training things
and I look for things that will impact how I can make
    training

better.

So I started seeing a lot of incidents similar to Rodney King
and some of them identical to Rodney King
and I said we gotta find some alternative uses of force.
And their attitude was:
"Don't worry about it,
don't worry about it."
And I said, "Wait a minute,
you gonna get some policemen indicted,
you gonna get some policemen sent to jail,
and they're gonna hurt somebody and it's gonna be
    perceived to be
other than a proper use of force,
and then you guys in management are gonna scurry away
    from it,
you're gonna run away from it,
you're gonna get somebody . . . somebody
is gonna go to the joint because of your lack of effort."
And the last conversation I had was with one of my . . .
He walked by my office,
so I ran out of my office and I catch up with him right by
    the
fountain,
right by where the water is.
I said,
"Listen, we got another one of these . . .
we gotta explore some techniques and we gotta explore
    some options,"
and his response to me:
"Sergeant Duke,
I'm tired of hearing this shit.

We're gonna beat people into submission
and we're gonna break bones."
And he said the Police Commission and the City Council
    took this
away from us.
"Do you understand that,
Sergeant Duke?"
And I said, "Yes, sir,"
and I never brought it up again.
And that, to me,
tells me
this is an "in your face" to the City Council and to the
    Police
Commission.
And like I said,
I can't prove this,
but I believe that Daryl Gates
and the Command staff were gonna do an "in your face" to
    the City
Council and the Police Commission, saying,
"You took upper-body-control holds away from us.
Now we're really gonna show you what you're gonna get,
with lawsuits and all the other things that are associated with it."

Indelible Substance

Josie Morales Clerk-typist, city
of Los Angeles uncalled witness to Rodney
King beating, Simi Valley trial

(In a conference room at her workplace, downtown
Los Angeles)

We lived in Apartment A6,
right next to A8,
which is where George Holliday lived.
And, um,
the next thing we know is, um,
ten or twelve officers made a circle around him
and they started to hit him.
I remember
that they just not only hit him with sticks,
they also kicked him,
and one guy,
one police officer, even pummeled his fist
into his face,
and they were kicking him.
And then we were like "Oh, my goodness,"
and I was just watching.
I felt like "Oh, my goodness"
'cause it was really like
he was in danger there,
it was such
an oppressive atmosphere.
I knew it was wrong—

whatever he did—
I knew it was wrong,
I just knew in my heart
this is wrong—
you know they can't do that.
And even my husband was petrified.
My husband said, "Let's go inside."
He was trying to get me to come inside
and away from the scene,
but I said, "No."
I said, "We have to stay here
and watch
because this is wrong."
And he was just petrified—
he grew up in another country where this is prevalent,
police abuse is prevalent in Mexico—
so we stayed and we watched the whole thing.
And
I was scheduled to testify
and I was kind of upset at the outcome,
because I had a lot to say
and during the trial I kept in touch with the
prosecutor,
Terry White,
and I was just very upset
and I, um,
I had received a subpoena
and I told him, "When do you want me to go?"
He says, "I'll call you later and I'll give you a time."
And the time came and went and he never called me,
so I started calling him.

I said, "Well, are you going to call me or not?"
And he says, "I can't really talk to you
and I don't think we're going to be using you because
it contradicts what Melanie Singer said."
And I faxed him a letter
and I told him that those officers were going to be acquitted
and one by one I explained these things to him in this letter
and I told him, "If you do not put witnesses,
if you don't put one resident and testify to say what they
    saw,"
And I told him in the letter
that those officers were going to be acquitted.
But I really believe that he was dead set
on that video
and that the video would tell all,
but, you see, the video doesn't show you where those
    officers went
and assaulted Rodney King at the beginning.
You see that?
And I was so upset. I told my co-worker, I said, "I had a
    terrible dream
that those guys were acquitted."
And she goes, "Oh no, they're not gonna be acquitted."
She goes, "You, you,
you know, don't think like that."
I said, "I wasn't thinking I had a dream!"
I said, "Look at this,
they were,
they were acquitted."
Yeah, I do have dreams
that come true,

but not as vivid as that one.
I just had this dream and in my heart felt . . .
and I saw the
men
and it was in the courtroom and I just
had it in my heart . . .
something is happening
and I heard they were acquitted,
because dreams are made of some kind of indelible
    substance.
And my co-worker said, "You shouldn't think like this,"
and I said, "I wasn't thinking
it was a dream."
And that's all,
and it came to pass.

Your Heads in Shame

Anonymous Man Juror in Simi Valley trial

(A house in Simi Valley. Fall. Halloween decorations are up. Dusk. Low lamplight. A slender, soft-spoken man in glasses. His young daughter and wife greeted me as well. Quietness.)

As soon as we went
into the courtroom with the verdicts
there were
plainclothes policemen everywhere.
You know, I knew that
there would be people unhappy with the verdict,
but I didn't expect near
what happened.
If I had known
what was going to happen,
I mean, it's not,
it's not fair to say I would have voted a different
way.
I wouldn't have—
that's not our justice system—
but I would have written a note to the judge saying,
"I can't do this,"
because of
what it put my family through.
Excuse me.
(Crying)
So anyway,

we started going out to the bus
and the police said
right away,
"If there's rocks and bottles, don't worry
the glass on the bus is bulletproof."
And then I noticed a huge mob scene,
and it's a sheriff's bus that they lock prisoners in.
We got to the hotel and there were some obnoxious
    reporters out
there
already, trying to get interviews.
And, you know, the police were trying to get us into the bus
    and cover
our faces,
and,
and this reporter said,
"Why are you hiding your heads in shame? Do you know
    that buildings
are burning
and people are dying in South LA
because of you?"
And twenty minutes later I got home
and the same obnoxious reporter was at the door
and my wife was saying, "He doesn't want to talk to
    anybody,"
and she kept saying,
"The people wanna know,
the people wanna know,"
and trying to get her foot in the door.
And I said, "Listen, I don't wanna talk to anybody. My wife
    has made

that clear."
And I,
you know, slammed the door in her face.
And so she pulled two houses down
and started
filming our house.
And watching on the TV
and seeing all the political leaders,
Mayor Bradley
and President Bush,
condemning our verdicts.
I mean, the jurors as a group, we tossed around:
was this a setup of some sort?
We just feel like we were pawns that were thrown away by
    the
system.
I mean,
the judge,
most of the jurors
feel like when he was reading the verdicts
he . . .
we thought we could sense a look of disdain on his face,
and he also had said
beforehand
that after the verdicts came out
he would like to come up and talk to us,
but after we gave the verdicts
he sent someone up and said he didn't really want to
do that then.
And plus, he had the right and power to
withhold our names for a period of time

and he did not do that,
he released them right away.
I think it was apparent that we would be harassed
and I got quite a few threats.
I got threatening letters and threatening phone calls.
I think he just wanted to separate himself . . .
A lot of newspapers published our addresses too.
The New York *Times* published the values of our homes.
They were released in papers all across the country.
We didn't answer the phone,
because it was just every three minutes . . .
We've been portrayed as white racists.
One of the most disturbing things, and a lot of the jurors
said that
the thing that bothered them that they received in the mail
more
than anything else,
more than the threats, was a letter from the KKK
saying,
"We support you, and if you need our help, if you want to
    join
our organization,
we'd welcome you into our fold."
And we all just were:
No, oh!
God!

Magic
Gil Garcetti District attorney

(Gil Garcetti came into office as district attorney of
Los Angeles in 1992. He followed Ira Reiner, who
had been in office during the unrest. He is a very
handsome man with prematurely white hair and a
lot of energy. He is in very good physical shape.
We met one morning in his office. It is a large,
brightly lit, immaculately kept office with a good
view. The seal of the state of California is behind
his desk as well as an American flag and the flag of
the state of California. He is wearing a bright-
colored tie. The head of public relations, Suzanne
Childs, sat in on the interview. She was an elegant,
simply dressed attractive blond woman. Both she
and Mr. Garcetti were very upbeat, friendly people.
We met in the spring of 1993.)

It goes back to what I said about jurors.
Much to most people's surprise,
they really very seriously take their oath.
For the most part
thee [sic]
the burden of proof in most criminal cases
is really extremely high,
and if you take it seriously, your oath seriously,
you really have to look at it.
I mean, you really have to look carefully at the evidence.
For the most part people have a respect for police,
even people who are annoyed by police.
At least in a courtroom setting
that magic comes in.
You want to believe the officers,

because they are there to help you,
the law-abiding citizen,
because most jurors have not had contacts
with police—
if they have
it's a traffic ticket
or they did a sloppy job
investigating their burglary
but not enough that it sours them on the police.
They are still there to help
and to protect you.
That's what we've been sold all our lives,
so when an officer comes in
and tells you
something from the witness stand
there is something magic
that comes over that individual
as opposed to you or Suzanne or me,
uh, going to testify.
And perhaps—
this is my trial experience . . .
seen it . . .
and it can be dispelled very easily.
I mean, if a cop, for example, comes in with a raid jacket
and guns bulging out
he'll wipe himself out very quickly,
because he'll look like he's a cowboy.
But if you have a man coming in
or a woman coming in—
you know, professionally dressed,
polite

with everyone—
the magic
is there
and it's a . . .
it's an aura,
it's aye [sic] feeling
that is conveyed to the jury:
"I am telling the truth
and I'm here to help you,
to protect you,"
and they want to believe that,
especially today they want to believe it,
because everyone is living
in a state of fear,
everyone.
I think you're seeing across the country
the credibility of the police
is
more uncertain,
but still for the most part
people want to believe the police officers
and do believe the police officers
unless the police officer
himself
or herself
gives 'em reason not to.
But you walk in with magic
and only you can destroy that magic.

Hammer
Stanley K. Sheinbaum Former
president, Los Angeles Police Commission

(A beautiful house in Brentwood. There is art on all
the walls. The art has a real spirit to it. It is the art of
his wife, Betty Sheinbaum. There is a large living
room, an office off the living room which you can
see. It is mostly made of wood, lots of papers and
books. The office of a writer. There are glass windows that look out on a pool, a garden, a view.
Behind us is a kitchen where his wife, Betty, was,
but she eventually left. Stanley is sitting at a round
wooden table with a cup of coffee. He is in a
striped shirt and khaki pants and loafers. He has a
beard. He is tall, and about seventy-three years
old. He seems gruff, but when he smiles or laughs,
his face lights up the room. It's very unusual. He
has the smile and laugh of a highly spiritual, joyous
old woman, like a grandmother who has really
been around. There is a bird inside the house who
occasionally chirps.)

Is this on on?
Is this tape on now?
Uh.
In the middle of the afternoon
I was at a lawyer's office in West LA.
Uh.
Then when I heard about the verdict—
which was not until about five-thirty,
'cause I was just,
y'know, wasn't a radio or TV—
I immediately headed downtown.

When
I got down to Parker Center,
or on the way down, I heard it on the radio,
and I had one interesting mini-experience
that told me there was gonna be trouble—
very simple thing.
As I was driving down the Santa Monica Freeway
there was a,
uh,
nice black recent BMW,
small car,
in good shape,
and there was an Afro-ican,
uh,
African-American woman
driving it,
and a man
next to her,
also African-American,
and she . . .
her window was open.
As she was driving,
she had a hammer in her hand,
and this was a very
dramatic thing,
in a minor way,
and it said to me:
trouble.
As I pulled into the garage—
and it's now
close to

six-thirty—
there's Daryl Gates
getting into his car,
and I ask him,
"Where you goin'?"
"I got something I gotta do."
That was the only answer I got.
As you may have heard,
turned out
that he was
on his way to a fund-raiser
up here,
two blocks over from here,
where he was lobbying,
campaigning against Prop.
F,
which I assume I don't have to give you the details.
The heart of Prop. F
is that it limits the chief's terms to five years,
with one renewable.
Under the old charter
the chief was in for perpetuity.
In the meantime,
after he heads out,
I get through with that
wondering what the hell
was going on with him.
He's the chief and this thing
very well
may be falling apart.
I start drifting around the department

and I heard screams down the hall.
Now, we have a bunch of people
working for the commission,
mainly women,
and it's seven o'clock already,
and a scream:
"They're coming in!"
I don't know if you want this kind of detail.
So I then went out toward the front
and there are plate-glass panes up above,
maybe seven or ten feet high,
and a rock comes through . . .

Characters

"Twilight Bey"

Jay Thompson

"Reginald Denny"

"Big Al"

"Stanley Sheinbaum"

Jim McHugh-Outline

"Katie Miller"

"Theresa Alison"

"Angela King"

"Anonymous Man #2" (Hollywood Agent)

"Sergeant Charles Duke"

"Elaine Brown"

"Mrs. Young-Soon Han"

War Zone

Riot

Chung Lee President of the Korean-American Victims Association

(A conference room in an office in Korea town. A
man in his sixties. His son translates. Afternoon.
The following is a phonetic transcription.*)

guda-ume o, uri,
gage ne-ibohant'e jonhwaha nikkani,
o, uri gugagega da t'olligo
guyangbanhanun, gusaramhanun yegiga

(And next I called my neighbor's store
and the gentleman—uh, the man told me,
"Your store's been completely looted!)

nohi mulgoni gilgonnos'o p'uraja-e jonbuda,
ap'e p'urajande p'urajallo jonbuda
gonnowa itta hanun jonhwarul badas' o,

(Your whole stock is scattered all over
in front of the project across the street.")

gunyang da ijen, o,
p'okttong-i nassunikkani,
mulgoni gocchok waitta goredo urin
gogi-e dehan-gon hanna
miryonhanna an-gajottagu

* Phonetics arranged by Kyung Ja Lee.

. . .

(Well now, uh . . .
I realized then that a riot had begun,
so even though our stuff was thrown out there,
we decided to give up
any sense of attachment to our possessions.)

guldoni e, gusaram hant'e
yolttushi ban-gyony-in-ga yolttushin-ga,
nohi gagega bult'ago ittago jonhwaga wattago yo

(And then, uh, he called around twelve-thirty or maybe
    twelve,
and he told me that my store was on fire.)

Messages

Tom Bradley Former mayor of the city of Los Angeles

(Fall, afternoon. His office at City Hall. He is in an armchair, I am on a sofa. It is a large office. A woman from the public relations office is there during the interview. He is dressed in a suit and tie. He entered the room after I had arrived, briskly and energetically. He has very long legs and sits with them outstretched, and his hands clasped to the side.)

I was in my office in City Hall.
We had
already decided on
a strategy and, uh,
an appeal to the press to
go live with a statement
at about 5 P.M. that day.
We learned that the verdict was coming in that afternoon.
Um,
we had four messages, depending on the verdict.
If it was
a guilty verdict, it was one message.
If it was a partial verdict,
some guilty, some not guilty, we had a separate message.
The one that I had put down as just a . . . a precautionary
    measure,
an acquittal on all counts,
was something
we

didn't seriously think could happen,
but we had a message
and it did happen.
And so within a matter of an hour and a half we had that
    message on
the air,
uh, directly to the public,
and it was essentially to call for . . . to express my outrage
at this verdict of
not guilty for all of these officers,
but to say to people
we've come too far
to make changes and to make progress.
Let us not
kill that effort by reacting with violence.
Speak your . . . your heart,
say what you feel
in terms of your dissatisfaction with the jury verdict
and the fact that it simply appeared to be something
    completely, uh,
completely
disconnected with the TV shots that you saw,
but say so . . .
do it in a verbal fashion
and don't engage in violence.

"Don't Shoot"

Richard Kim Appliance store owner

(Morning. August 1993. A Korean-American man in his thirties. He is dressed in khakis, a white shirt, and a tie. We are sitting in the back of his electronics store, which is quite large. We are in a room with very expensive stereo equipment.)

We waited for about half an hour
and then my father showed up with a neighbor.
He told me what had happened.
There was no police officer to be found anywhere.
We came back here.
We started calling all the police stations and the hospitals to
    see if
anybody had checked in
if they fit the description.
Unfortunately we can't get any kind of answer from anybody.
While that was happening, a neighbor called and said you
    better
come down here because
there are hundreds of people and your store's being looted
at this time.
So we packed up our van, four people, five people, including
myself, and we headed down there.
I already knew people were carrying guns,
already knew my mother was shot at that corner.
So it was like going to war.
That's the only thing I can say.
By the time we got there

at this time
there are hundreds of people at our store.
At that time when we were approaching the store
I realized there are gunshots going on.
As I was approaching the store
one person was carrying to the side—
obviously he was wounded—
and our neighbor,
he was a car dealership and he was trying to hold down the
    store,
trying to keep the people back,
and I can see one person still at the corner by the door
with a shotgun and I looked at across the street.
There are at least three or four people with handguns firing
    back.
There was exchange of fire going on.
So I pulled our van—I was driving—
I pulled our van in between our store entrance,
in between the person firing at me in front of the store,
and I got out and my first thought was I could use the van
    to block
the bullets from hitting the guy in front of the store.
I yelled for everybody to stop shooting, yelled,
"Don't shoot!"
For a split second, they stopped shooting.
And across the street
I looked, could see three people, they looked at me, and
    they pointed the
guns at me.
And they were so close
I could see the barrels of the guns.

And . . . I knew they were going to start firing.
I got a gut feeling.
And I ducked.
And . . . they started firing at the van.
And . . . I came around the van, to the back.
And . . . we had a rifle inside the van.
And . . . I pulled it out,
pulled the trigger,
and it just clicked, because there was no bullet in the
   chamber.
So I went back,
put the bullet in the chamber, and returned fire at the
   people firing
at us.
I wasn't aiming to hurt anybody.
More or less trying to disperse the people.
I was firing at the general direction that the gunfire was
   coming from.
When that happened, people dispersed.
I guess the people firing at me decided it wasn't worth it
   and they all
took off.
Everybody just went "pa-chew."

Butta Boom

Joe Viola Television writer

(A friendly man, in an area between Beverly Hills and Mid-Wilshire. We are sitting in a very bright room, almost like a covered patio. He has set out cheese and fruit and crackers for us. He is in a pair of jeans, a striped cotton shirt, and wears his glasses on his forehead.)

The, the bottom line is . . .
is that
I believe that
there is extraordinary justice.
Not that it happens day in and day out,
but *our* court
the real court
where *we* judged these cases,
where I experienced the riots, where my family did,
for the first time
in my entire life,
my entire life,
I was terrified.
'Cause I sat here.
It began at the corner of the Big Five.
I was standing there,
just having mailed my daughter's registration to Berkeley,
    what
better stroke,
and I was standing there when the first cars rolled by and
    this was

like one-thirty in the afternoon,
and they . . . I saw a kid with a nine
and he brought it up,
he didn't aim it directly at me but he said,
"I'm goin' to kill you, motherfucker,"
or "You're dead, motherfucker."
Something like that.
Right *here*, right on the corner!
I sat back down like my ass was filled with cement,
right on the corner,
right here, "butta boom."
And when they pulled into the Big Five lot
at that time, moments before,
I heard screams
and I started to cross the street.
It's a three-way
and I looked down toward the Jewish Federation, and I
    didn't see it.
Didn't see anything happening.
That's when these cars rolled up.
Exactly a week later, in the LA *Times* was this unbelievable
    story
about . . . that these two cars pulled to the curb
and a girl—there were three teenage girls in the first car—
got out of the car with a two-by-four
and smacked the guy right in the head, smacked him right
    in the
head!
Did you hear this story?
Young guy, briefcase, regular West
Side attaché carrier.

This was lunchtime, one-thirty,
and the guy dropped the case,
blood in his face,
disoriented, started walking
toward the car and the curb.
Now people were screaming, "No, no, no."
And this one girl,
black,
a dancer
out of work for a week doing temp work,
was going to an office job.
She's been called
and she was just going to work, she had an address.
She sees this white guy with the blood in his face.
She runs over to him
to pull him away.
Now, the Jewish Federation has all these ex-Israeli
    commandos
as security,
so this guy who was in the lobby
heard the screams and came running out and he's got a
    nine-millimeter
himself.
One of the guys in the car says to the kid in the passenger
    seat,
"Shoot 'em!"
And so he shot the girl,
shot her through the leg!
This is one you ought to track down!
He took a piece of her calf out.
So—this was two minutes later—

that car came up to me.
Anyway, the next thing I know
they pulled into the Big Five, and I'm running.
I come running in. I said,
"Marsha,
shut the doors.
I'm going in to go get the kids."

War Zone

Judith Tur Ground reporter, LA News
Service

(The Santa Monica Airport. A small airport. Their
hangar. Lunchtime. Judy is a very, very attractive
woman in her fifties. She is blond. She is impecca-
bly made up. She is wearing black tights, a white
T-shirt, or long white jersey. She has on black
suede cowboy boots with high heels. She has a
tan. Planes are heard during this interview. We are
sitting in front of a television. She is showing me the
video which John and Marika Tur took from their
helicopter over Florence and Normandie. This was
the famous video of the Reginald Denny beating.)

This is the beginning of the riots
and, uh,
this is the video we're going to be giving you for your show.
Here's a gang member.
Here . . .
This is
a live broadcast, by the way.
Now watch this, Anna.
This is absolutely,
I think,
disgraceful.
These poor . . .
He fell like a sack of potatoes.
I mean, real brave men, right?
Now these women here—
you'll see them later—

are taking pictures of this.
This is sick.
So this is the video I'm gonna be . . .
that I'm gonna give you for the show.
I'm gonna fast-forward here,
because you can see him
getting up
and nobody's helping him.
These two
men try to help
him.
Football
tells them something.
"Get away."
Okay?
Look at this
decrepit old man
and look at these,
these clowns
here.
Anybody with any kind
of a heart would go over and try and help.
Here's Reginald Denny passing by.
If you saw an animal being beaten, you would go over and
     help an
animal.
Okay, here's a black man
going and helping.
I think his name is, um,
Larry
Tarvo.

T-a-r-v-o.

And this gentleman here is getting his glasses and trying to
    help him

and . . .

He risked his life doing that.

Now you'll see Reginald Denny

and I look at this and each time I see this

I get angrier and angrier.

Because there was no reason for this to have happened.

*(You can hear John talking throughout very faintly from the
helicopter about what we are seeing, you hear a very clear "Oh
my God" from Marika again. It is them talking to police
helicopters, etc., which came out on the video.)*

Okay, here's another animal

videotaping this guy.

These people have no heart.

These people don't deserve

to live.

Sorry for getting emotional,

but I mean this is not my United States anymore.

This is sicko.

Did you see him shoot him?

Did you see that?

(Rewinds the tape)

This is like being in a war zone.

This is the guy with the gun.

Pulls out the rifle.

You see

the shot?

He missed Reginald Denny.

He missed him.

But he doesn't even run across the street.
You would think he would want to run
and disappear.
As far as I'm concerned,
nobody is better than me,
I'm not better than anybody else.
People are people.
Black, white, green, or purple, I don't care,
but what's happening in South-Central now,
I think they're really taking advantage.
Now I'm mad,
and you know what?
Let them go out and work for a living.
I'm sick of it.
We've all had a rough time in our life.
I've had major rough time.
At forty-two years old
I left my husband.
Never got a divorce 'cause he died four months later.
You know what Judy Tur did?
I used to be a clothing manufacturer.
My husband was major gambler,
blew everything.
I was penniless.
I got a job from ten until three in the afternoon working in
    a doctor's
office making minimum
and from four until midnight every day
worked in a market as a cashier.
I mean, from living on Bel Air Road to . . .
I hadda do it.

And you know what?

It embarrassed me when people said, "What are you doing
    at the

market?"

I was like it was so beneath me.

And now when I run into those people

I'm proud of what I did.

But I would never think of going on welfare.

I would never think of robbing a market,

holding

somebody at gunpoint.

I hate guns.

But you know what?

I don't hate them anymore.

If I'm threatened, my life is threatened, I'm not even

going,

going to hesitate.

I pull that trigger if my life is threatened.

It's terrible for me to be angry—

I hate to be angry—

and what's happening, the white people are getting so angry
    now

that they're going back fifty years instead of being pushed
    ahead.

Bubble Gum Machine Man
Allen Cooper, a.k.a. Big Al

Ex-gang member, ex-convict, activist in
national truce movement

(He is wearing an odd cap with a button, and buttons on his shirt. In a gym in Nickerson Gardens, 5:30 P.M.)

The L.A. Four they committed a crime of what?
Assault
and battery?
And what did the government dig for?
What did they dig for?
Stoppin' traffic of a truck?
Are they sure that truck belonged in that area?
Did they check to see if that truck qualified to fit on that
    city street?
No, they didn't check that.
That wasn't a highway or nothin';
that was a boulevard.
He was turnin' off a residential street!
You gotta understand, it may have been a
intimidation move,
OK,
drivin' into a location that is at a uprising.
And I guess he's at a point tryin' to prove he can get
past.
Any other commonsense person

woulda went around.
But we're not basin' our life on Reginald Denny;
neither are we basin' our lives on Rodney King.
Only thing we're expressing through the Rodney King—
through Reginald Denny beating—
it shows how
a black person gets treated in his community.
And it was once brought to the light
and shown
and then we still . . . we see no belief,
because they never handled, from the top of the level, the
    way it
should have been handled,
because they handled like a soap opera.
That's all that
really was.
If you put twenty hidden cameras
in the country jail system,
you got people beat worse than that
point blank.
Some jails got things
called
the red room
and the blue room,
you get what they call an attitude adjustment.
What Rodney King . . .
It been—
it's been twenty, thirty years,
and people suffered beatings from law enforcement.
It ain't nothin' new.
It was just brought to the light this time.

But then it showed what—
it showed that it doesn't mean a thing,
It doesn't mean a thing.
Now if that was an officer down there gettin' beat,
it would a been a real national riot thing—
you hear me?
Just imagine how many people woulda been out there
clappin';
it wouldn't a been no sad sorry, hot . . .
it woulda been a happy hot line.
Everybody makin' emotion out of somethin':
Rotney King, Rotney King, Rotney King.
It's not Rotney King.
It's the ghetto.
I was at one of these swap meets
and a bubble gum machine man pulled a gun out.
Now what a bubble gum machine man doin' with a pistol?
Who wanna rob a bubble gum machine?
Because we live here, the conditions are so
enormous and so dangerous,
that they have to be qualified to carry a firearm.
What is the purpose?
You got to live here to express this point, you got to live
here to see what's goin' on.
You gotta look at history, baby,
you gotta look at history.
It wasn't . . .
Anything is never a problem 'til the black man gets his
        hands on it.
It was good for the NRA
to have fully automatic weapons,

but when the Afro-American people got hold of 'em,
it was a crime!
Aww . . .
He's a problem
in the neighborhood;
he has a AK-47 assault weapon.
We didn't bring them guns here.
We didn't make up—
they was put here for a reason:
to entrap us!
Point blank.
You gotta look at history, baby,
you gotta look at history.
This Reginald Denny thing is a joke.
It's joke.
That's just a delusion to the real
problem.

A Weird Common Thread in Our Lives

Reginald Denny

(In the office of Johnnie Cochran, his lawyer. A
conference room. Walls are lined with law books.
Denny is wearing a baseball hat and T-shirt. His
friend, a man, is there with a little girl. One of
Cochran's assistants, a young black woman attorney, sits in on the interview. Denny is upbeat,
speaks loudly. Morning, May 1993.)

Every single day
I must make this trip to Inglewood—no problem—
and I get off the freeway like usual,
taking up as much space as I can in the truck.
People don't like that.
Because I have to.
That little turn onto Florence
is pretty tricky,
it's really a tight turn.
I take two lanes to do it in
and
it was just like a scene
out of a movie.
Total confusion and chaos.
I was just in awe.
And the thing that I remember most vivid—
broken glass
on the ground.
And for a split second I was goin'

check this out,
and the truck in front of me—
and I found out later—
the truck in front of me,
medical supplies goin' to Daniel Freeman!
(He laughs)
Kind of a
ironic thing!
And the, uh,
the strange thing was
that what everyone thought was a fire extinguisher
I got clubbed with,
it was a bottle of oxygen,
'cause the guy had medical supplies.
I mean,
does anyone know
what a riot looks like?
I mean, I'm sure they do now.
I didn't have a clue of what one looked like
and
I didn't know that the verdict had come down.
I didn't pay any attention
to that,
because that
was somebody else's problem
I guess I thought
at the time.
It didn't have anything to do with me.
I didn't usually pay too much attention of what was going on
    in
California

or in America or anything
and, uh,
I couldn't for the life of me figure out what was goin' on.
Strange things do happen on that street.
Every now and again police busting somebody.
That was a street that was never . . .
I mean, it was always an exciting . . .
we,
lot of guys looked forward to going down that street
'cause there was always something going on, it seemed
like,
and the cool thing was I'd buy those cookies
from
these guys
on the corner,
and I think they're, uh,
Moslems?
And they sell cookies
or cakes,
the best-tasting stuff,
and whatever they were selling that day,
and it was always usually a surprise,
but it was very well known
that it was a good surprise!
Heck, a good way to munch!
But when I knew something was wrong was when they
    bashed in the
right window of
my truck.
That's the end of what I remember as far as anything
until five or six days later.

They say I was in a coma.
And I still couldn't figure out,
you know,
how I got here.
And
It was quite a few weeks after I was in the hospital
that they even let on that there was a riot,
because the doctor didn't feel it
was something I needed to know.
Morphine is what they were givin me for pain,
and it was just an interesting time.
But I've never been in an operating room.
It was like . . .
this is just . . .
I 'member like in a movie
they flip on the big lights
and they're really in there.
(He laughs)
I was just goin' "God"
and seein' doctors around with masks on
and I still didn't know why I was still there
and next thing
I know I wake up a few days later.
I think when it really dawned on me
that something big might have happened
was when important people wanted to come in and say hi.
The person that I remember that wanted to come in and see me,
the first person that I was even aware of who wanted to see me,
was Reverend Jesse Jackson,
and I'm just thinkin':
not this guy,

that's the dude I see on TV all the time.
And then it was a couple days later that
Arsenio Hall came to see me
and he just poked his head in, said hello,
and, uh,
I couldn't say nothin' to him.
And then, about then I started to, uh,
started to get it.
And by the time I left Daniel Freeman I knew what
    happened,
except they wouldn't let me watch it on TV.
I mean, they completely controlled that remote-control
    thing.
They just had it on a movie station.
And if I hadn't seen some of the stuff,
you know, of me doin' a few things after everything was
    done,
like climbing back into the truck,
and talking to Titus and Bobby and Terry and Lee—
that's the four people
who came to my rescue,
you know—they're telling me stuff that I would never
even have known.
Terry
I met only because she came as a surprise guest visit to the
    hospital.
That was an emotional time.
How does one say that
someone
saved
my life?

How does a person,
how do I
express enough
thanks
for someone risking their
neck?
And then I was kind of . . .
I don't know if "afraid" is the word,
I was just a little,
felt a little awkward meeting people
who
saved me.
Meeting them was not like meeting
a stranger,
but it was like
meeting a
buddy.
There was a weird common thread in our lives
That's an extraordinary event,
and here is four people—
the ones in the helicopter—
and they just stuck with it,
and then you got four people
who seen it on TV
and said enough's enough
and came to my rescue.
They tell me
I drove the truck for what? About a hundred or so feet.
The doctors say there's *fight* or *flight* syndrome.
And I guess I was in *flight!*
And it's been seventeen years since I got outta high school!

I been driving semis,
it's almost second nature,
but Bobby Green
saw that I was gettin' nowhere fast and she just jumped in and
scooted me over
and drove the truck.
By this time
it was tons of glass and blood everywhere,
'cause I've seen pictures of what I looked like
when I first went into surgery,
and I mean it was a pretty
bloody mess.
And they showed me my hair,
when they cut off my hair
they gave it to me in a plastic bag.
And it was just
long hair and
glass and blood.
Lee—
that's a woman—
Lee Euell,
she told me
she just
cradled me.
There's no
passenger seat in the truck
and here I am just kind of on my knees in the middle of the floor
and, uh,
Lee's just covered with blood,

and Titus is on one side,
'cause Bobby couldn't see out the window.
The front windshield was so badly broken
it was hard to see.
And Titus is standing on the running board telling Bobby
    where to go,
and then Terry,
Titus's girlfriend,
she's in front of the truck
weaving through traffic,
dodging toward cars
to get them to
kind of move out of the way,
to get them to clear a path,
and next stop was
Daniel Freeman Hospital!
Someday when I,
uh,
get a house,
I'm gonna have one of the rooms
and it's just gonna be
of all the riot stuff
and it won't be a
blood-and-guts
memorial,
it's not gonna be a sad,
it's gonna be a happy room.
It's gonna be . . .
Of all the crazy things that I've got,
all the,
the

love and compassion
and the funny notes
and the letters from faraway places,
just framed, placed,
framed things,
where a person will walk in
and just have a good old time in there.
It'll just be
fun to be in there,
just like a fun thing,
and there won't be
a color problem
in this room.
You take the toughest
white guy
who thinks he's a bad-ass
and
thinks he's better than any other race in town,
get him in a position where he needs help,
he'll take the help
from no matter who the color of the guy across . . .
because he's so self-
centered and -serving,
he'll take it
and then
soon as he's better
he'll turn around
and rag on 'em.
I know that for a fact.
Give me what I need and shove off.
It's crazy, it's nuts.

That's the person I'd like to shake and go,
"Uuuh,
you fool,
you selfish little shit"—
those kind of words.
"Uhhh, man, you *nut*."
(Pause and intense stare, low-key)
I don't know what I want.
I just want people to wake up.
It's not a color, it's a person.
So this room,
it's just gonna be
people,
just a wild place,
it's gonna be a blast.
One day,
Lord
willing, it'll happen.

A Badge of Courage
Captain Lane Haywood

Compton Fire Department

> (Morning, August 1993. A fire station in Compton.
> Mr. Haywood is a tall, dark-skinned, muscular, at-
> tractive man, with a huge smile and a very positive
> manner. He is dressed in uniform. There were vari-
> ous sounds of the firehouse.)

So . . . it was just an enormous amount of fire.
It was just difficult for the amount of men that I have to
    completely
extinguish that fire.
So I made a decision to get to the ruf [sic],
cut a firebreak, and the firebreak is . . . is a gap
in the ruf that we cut in the ruf
between two adjoining buildings to try to stop the fire at
    that point.
And while we were up on the ruf, me and my firefighters,
we received gunfire.
Now, I don't know if it was directed at us, but, you know,
    when you're
up on the ruf
and you hear rat-tat-tat-tat, the first thing you do is you hit
    the
deck.
So we hit the deck.
And then I . . . I just give the word to
"Let's get down the ruf."
So we abandoned that

and got down the ruf,
came to find out later that it
was a gang of people on the back side
of the mall that were trying to rush the police,
who were trying to protect the fashion center.
And the police officers fired shots in the air to make them
    get back.
Needless to say, it took us a considerable amount of time
just to even get that fire under control.
And subsequently,
while we were fighting that fire . . .
You can see on Long Beach Boulevard
there's a Pep Boys across the street
and other stores throughout the boulevard.
You hear gunfire down the street
and the next thing you know
you see all these cars backing down the street,
tryin' to . . . you know, run.
And the police were there blockin' the street
and they didn't respond to the gunfire.
They just let people back out and tryin' to get away.
And at the same time, you had looters breakin' in,
breakin' the windows of Pep Boys,
tryin' to get in, *With the police there,*
you know, and the thought came to my mind is,
"Wow, this is ridiculous! Right in front of the police!"
And then . . .
and then shortly after that,
uh, the police on the back side of the mall . . .
'cause
there's Long Beach Boulevard and on the other street

to the east of that is
Bolis Road.
From Bolis Road you can drive naturally to the parking lot.
They redirected the traffic.
And they started coming through from the driveway to
    where we
were.
I tell you,
I've never seen so much anger and hostility in females.
In my life.
I mean, I dealt with that out in the street.
I've been here nineteen years. I mean
they're sitting in the windowsills,
both front and back windows of these cars
maybe sitting in the back
or in the beds of pickups,
driving through hollering a slogan,
"Let the motherfuckers burn."
There's another fire, cleaners,
barbershops, and a laundromat across the street.
That was fully involved.
And I looked up.
I saw a task force of engines
coming from Huntington Beach.
So . . . the task force,
they had three engines
and they had a battalion chief
and they had a police escort,
all white guys,
escorted in, and they had the name of the city,
and they had it blocked off with cardboard.

So they couldn't really tell what city it was from,
but in fire service you know who's who.
They, eh, had the protection,
they had the manning,
they had the equipment.
And they started to extinguish the fire across the street,
and I'm standing there with four guys
and this big old truck.
No help, no vests, no police,
no nothing.
And see, the irony of it is they had the vests for us.
Because what happened . . .
FBI, from what the police officers tell me,
pulled into the parking lot with a truckful of vests,
and all the police officers
and all the nonessentials grabbed 'em
and didn't notify the Fire Department
that they had vests.
See, our chief doesn't want us to wear vests because he
    claims it will
telegraph a message to the citizens that Compton is
    dangerous.
Bulletproof vests.
Now, he says that this is our vest—
our badges.
You see, you should have a vest, a badge of courage.
You see, it's not about courage.
When you hear gunfire, you know when you see it,
you're constantly ruling out individuals that are shot,
looking at the types of wounds, you know.
You don't want to be a part of that.

You know.
I have a responsibility to my family to come home.
I take the dangers that relate to fire and so forth,
the explosions,
the chemicals
that may be inside a building,
but the gunfire, you know,
that's not a part of this.

To Look Like Girls from Little

Elvira Evers General worker and
cashier, Canteen Corporation

(A Panamanian woman in a plaid shirt, in an apartment in Compton. Late morning, early afternoon.
She has a baby on her lap. The baby has earrings
in her ears. Elvira has a gold tooth. There is a four-
year-old girl with large braid on top of her head
and a big smile who is around throughout the interview. The girl's name is Nella.)

So
everybody was like with things they was takin',
like
a carnival,
and I say
to my friend Frances,
"Frances, you see this?"
and she said, "Girl, you should see
that
it's getting worst."
And I say, "Girl, let me take my butt
up there before something happen."
And, um,
when somebody throw a bottle
and I just . . .
then
I felt
like moist,

and it was like a tingling sensation—right?—
and I didn't like this,
and it was like itchin',
and I say, "Frances, I'm bleedin'."
And she walk with me to her house
And she say, "Lift up your gown, let me see."
She say, "Elvira, it's a bullet!"
I say, "What?"
I say, "I didn't heard nothin'."
She say, "Yes, but it's a bullet."
She say, "Lay down there. Let me call St. Francis and tell
    them that
you been shot
and to send an ambulance."
And she say,
"Why you?
You don't mess with none of those people.
Why they have to shoot you?"
So Frances say the ambulance be here in fifteen minutes.
I say, "Frances,
I cannot wait that."
I say,
"I'm gone!"
So I told my oldest son, I say,
"Amant, take care your brothers.
I be right back."
Well, by this time he was standing up there, he was crying,
all of them was crying.
What I did for them not to see the blood—
I took the gown and I cover it
and I didn't cry.

That way they didn't get nervous.
And I get in the car.
I was goin' to drive.
Frances say, "What you doin'?"
I said, "I'm drivin'."
She say, "No, you're not!"
And we take all the back streets
and she was so supportive,
because she say, "You all right?
You feel cold?
You feel dizzy?
The baby move?"
She say, "You nervous?"
I say, "No, I'm not nervous, I'm just worried about the
    baby."
I say, "I don't want to lose this baby."
She say, "Elvira, everything will be all right." She say, "Just
    pray."
So there was a lot of cars, we had to be blowing the horn.
So finally we get to St. Francis
and Frances told the front-desk office, she say,
"She been shot!"
And they say, "What she doin' walkin'?"
and I say, "I feel all right."
Everybody stop doin' what they was doin'
and they took me to the room
and put the monitor to see if the baby was fine
and they find the baby heartbeat,
and as long as I heard the baby heartbeat I calmed down,
long as I knew whoever it is, boy or girl, it's all right,
and

matter of fact, my doctor, Dr. Thomas, he was there
at
the emergency room.
What a coincidence, right?
I was just lookin' for that familiar face,
and soon as I saw him
I say, "Well I'm all right now."
Right?
So he bring me this other doctor and then told me,
"Elvira, we don't know how deep is the bullet.
We don't know where it went. We gonna operate on
you.
But since that we gonna operate we gonna take the baby out
and you don't have to
go through all of that."
They say, "Do you understand
what we're saying?"
I say, "Yeah!"
And they say, "Okay, sign here."
And I remember them preparing me
and I don't remember anything else.
Nella!
No.
(Turns to the side and admonishes the child)
She likes company.
And in the background
I remember Dr. Thomas say, "You have a six-pound-twelve-
   ounce little
girl."
He told me how much she weigh and her length
and he

say, "Um,
she born,
she had the bullet in her elbow,
but when we remove . . .
when we clean her up
we find out that the bullet was still between two joints,
so
we did operate on her and your daughter is fine
and you are fine."
(Sound of a little child saying "Mommy")
Nella!
She wants to show the baby.
Jessica,
bring the baby.
(She laughs)
Yes,
yes.
We don't like to keep the girls without earrings. We like the
    little
girls
to look like girls from little.
I pierce hers.
When I get out on Monday,
by Wednesday I did it,
so by Monday she was five days,
she was seven days,
and I
pierced her ears
and the red band is just like for evil eyes.
We really believe in Panama . . .
in English I can't explain too well.

And her doctor, he told . . .
he explain to me
that the bullet
destroyed the placenta
and went through
me
and she caught it in her arms.
(*Here you can hear the baby making noises, and a bell rings*)
If she didn't caught it in her arm,
me and her would be dead.
See?
So it's like
open your eyes,
watch what is goin' on.
(*Later in the interview, Nella gave me a bandaid, as a gift.*)

National Guard

Julio Menjivar Lumber salesman and driver

(Near South Central, beautiful birds, traffic, hammering. In a kind of patio outside the backyard. A covered patio. Saturday morning. Very sunny. We sit on a bench. His BMW in the background. A man from El Salvador, in his late twenties. Later his mother and grandmother come to be photographed with him.)

And then,
a police passed by
and said,
that's fine,
that's fine
that you're doing that.
Anyway,
it's your neighborhood.
They were just like laughing or I don't know—
LAPD.
Black and white.
They just passed by and said it
in the radio:
Go for it.
Go for it,
it's your neighborhood.
I was only standing there
watching what was
happening.

And then
suddenly
jeeps came
from everywhere,
from all directions,
to the intersection.
Trucks
and
the National Guard.
And they threw all of
the people on the ground.
They threw
everybody down
and I was
in the middle of
a group.
They lifted me by my
arm like this.
First he told me to get up.
He said ugly things to me.
And as you see,
I'm a little fat,
so I couldn't get up.
They called me stupid.
He said, said,
many ugly things.
He said,
"Get up motherfucker, get up. Get up!"
Then he kicked me in the back.
He said,
"Come on, fat fucker,

get up."
Then I heard my wife
and my father
calling my name,
"Julio, Julio, Julio."
And then
my mother
and my sister and my wife,
they tried to go to the corner
and my mother
They almost shoot
them, almost shot them.
They were
pissed off,
too angry.
The National Guard.
They almost shot
my mom,
my wife,
and my sister
for try . . .
They will ask everybody questions
and the other guys don't know how to speak English.
Then the police don't like that.
So slap 'em in the face—
that guy got slapped three times.
An RTD bus came
and parked here
in the street,
and they put all of
us on it.

They took us to a station,
Southwest.
Young people
that got arrested.
Uh,
there was this guy crying and this other guy crying
because too tight,
too tight
the handcuffs.
And I felt very bad,
very bad.
Never never
in my life have I
been arrested.
Never
in my life.
Not in El Salvador.
This is the first time
I been in jail.
I was real scared,
yeah, yeah.
'Cause you got all these criminals
over there.
I'm not a criminal.
It's a lot of crazy people out there,
too many.
So I sit down.
So I barely close my eyes
and they went back—
pow pow pow pow pow
come on come on get up get up

come on get up,
and they had us
on our knees
for two hours.
I was praying,
yeah,
I was praying, yeah.
Yeah, that's true
I was praying.
I was thinking of all the
bad that could happen.
Yeah.
Now I have a record.
Aha, and a two-hundred-fifty-dollar
fine
and probation for
three years.

That's Another Story

Katie Miller Bookkeeper and accountant

(South Central, September 1992. A very large
woman sitting in an armchair. She has a baseball
cap on her head. She speaks rapidly with great
force and volume.)

I think this thing
about the Koreans and the Blacks . . .
that wasn't altogether true,
and I think that the Korean stores
that got burned in the Black neighborhood that were
    Korean-owned,
it was due to lack of
gettin' to know
the people that come to your store—
that's what it is.
Now,
they talk about the looting
in Koreatown . . . those wasn't blacks,
those wasn't blacks, those was Mexicans
in Koreatown.
We wasn't over there lootin' over there,
lootin' over there,
but here,
in this right here.
The stores that got looted for this one reason
only is that . . . know who you goin' know,
just know people comin' to your store, that's all,

just respect people comin' in there—
give 'em their money
'stead of just give me your money and get out of my face.
And it was the same thing with the '65 riots,
same thing.
And this they kept makin' a big
the Blacks and the Koreans.
I didn't see that,
and now see like
Pep
Boys that right there . . .
I didn't like the idea of Pep Boys myself,
I didn't like the idea of them hittin' Pep
Boys.
Only reason I can think they hit 'em is they too damn
    high—
that's the only reason.
Other than that
I think that Pep Boys just
came, people say
to hell with Pep boys, Miney Mo and Jack.
Let me just go in here,
I'm get me some damn
whatever the hell they have in there.
Now, I didn't loot this time.
Get that out,
because in my mind it's more
than that,
you know.
But I didn't loot this time.
I was praising the ones that had,

you know,
you oughta burn that sucker down.
But after it was over,
we went touring,
call it touring,
all around,
and we went to that Magnin store,
seein' people comin' out of that Magnin store,
and I was so
damn mad at that Paul Moyer.
He's a damn newscaster.
He was on Channel 7,
now that sucker's on Channel 4,
makin' eight million dollars.
What the hell,
person can make eight million dollars for readin' a piece of
    paper,
but that's a different story.
Highest of any newscaster.
I don't know why.
To read some damn paper.
I don't give a damn who tells me the damn news,
long as they can talk,
long as I can understand 'em,
I don't care,
but that's a different story.
Anyway, we went to Magnin
and we seen people run in there and looted.
It's on Wilshire,
very exclusive store,
for very . . . you know,

you have to have money to go in there to buy something,
and the people I seen runnin' out there that didn't have
    money to buy . . .
And I turned on the TV
and here is Mr. Paul Moyer
saying,
"Yeah,
they, they, uh,
some people looted, uh,
I. Magnin.
I remember goin' to that store when I was a child."
What he call 'em?
He called 'em thugs,
these thugs goin' into that store.
I said, "Hell with you, asshole."
That was my, my . . .
I said, "Okay, okay for them to run into these other stores,"
you know,
"but don't go in no store
that I, I grew up on that has . . .
that my parents
took me
to that is
expensive—
these stores,
they ain't supposed to be, to be
looted.
How dare you loot a store
that rich people go to?
I mean, the nerve of them."
I found that very offensive.

Who the hell does he think he is?
Oh, but that was another story,
they lootin' over here,
but soon they loot this store he went to,
oh, he was all pissed.
It just made me sick,
but that's another story too.

Godzilla
Anonymous Man #2 (Hollywood Agent)

(Morning. A good looking man in shirt and tie and
fine shoes. A chic office in an agency in Beverly
Hills. We are sitting in a sofa.)

There was still the uneasiness that was growing
when the fuse was still burning,
but
it was
business as usual.
Basically,
you got
such-and-so on line one,
such-and-so on line two.
Traffic,
Wilshire,
Santa Monica.
Bunch of us hadda go to lunch at the
the Grill
in Beverly Hills.
Um,
gain major
show business dead center business restaurant,
kinda loud but genteel.
The . . . there was an incipient panic—
you could just feel—
the tension

in the
restaurant
it
was palpable,
it was tangible,
you could cut it with a knife.
All anyone was talking
about, you could hear little bits
of information—
did ya hear?
did ya hear?
It's like we were transmitting
thoughts
to each other
all across the restaurant,
we were transmitting thoughts to each other.
All the,
frankly, the
white
upper class,
upper middle class—
whatever your,
the
definition is—
white successful . . .
spending too much money,
too, ya know, too good a restaurant,
that kinda thing.
We were just
getting ourselves into a frenzy,
which I think a lot of it

involved
guilt,
just generic guilt.
When we drove back,
and it's about a ten-minute drive,
talking about the need
for guns
to protect ourselves,
it had just gone from there to there.
But I'm tellin' you, nothin' happened!
I don't mean somebody in the restaurant
had a fight
or somebody screamed at someone—
nothing, just,
ya know,
Caesar salad,
da-de-da,
ya know,
but the whole
bit
went
like that.
We walked in
from the underground garage into here and we looked at
     each other
and we could see people
running around
instead of . . . like,
people walk fast in this business
but now they were, they were like
running,

and
we looked at ourselves—
"we gotta close the office."
So we had gone from
"I'm a little nervous"
to "We gotta close the office,
shut down."
This is a business
we don't shut down.
Memo goes
out saying:
"Office closed for the day.
Everyone please leave
the office."
And *then*
I remember somebody said:
"Did you hear?
They're burning down
the Beverly Center."
By the way, *they* . . .
No no no, it's . . .
There is no *who*.
Whaddya mean, *who*?
No, just *they*.
That's fair enough.
"Did you hear *they* are burning down the Beverly Center?"
Oh, okay, *they* . . .
Ya know what I mean?
It almost didn't matter who,
it's irrelevant.
*Somebo*dy.

It's not *us*!
That was one of the highlights for me.
So I'm looking outside
and the traffic is far worse
and people were basically fleeing the office
and we were closing all the blinds
and this is about,
um,
I guess about four o'clock.
The vision of all these yuppies
and aging or aged yuppies,
Armani suits,
and, you know,
fleeing like
wild-eyed . . .
All you needed was Godzilla behind them,
you know,
like this . . .
chasing them out of the building,
that's really it.
Aaah, aaah.
(He laughs, a very hearty laugh)
Still,
still,
nothing had happened—
I don't mean to tell you that bombs were exploding—
nothing, zero.
So we,
I was one of the last to leave,
as usual,
and the roads were so packed it

it must be like
they were leaving
Hiroshima
or something,
Dresden . . .
I've never been in a war or . . .
just the daily war of . . .
(Intercom beeps)
Who's that?
Do you need me?
One sec. *(He leaves, then returns)*
Where was I?
Yeah.
What, what was, was
"I deserve it,"
you know,
was I, was I getting
my . . .
when I was *fearing*
for
safety
or my family or something . . .
those moments.
Because the panic was so high
that, oh my God,
I was almost thinking:
"Did I deserve this,
do I, do I deserve it?"
I thought me, personally—no,
me, generically,
maybe so.

Even though I, I . . .
what's provoked it—
the spark—
was the verdict,
which was
ab*surd.*
But that was just the spark—
this had been set
for years before.
But maybe,
not maybe,
but, uh, the
system
plays unequally,
and the people who were
the, they,
who were burning down the Beverly Center
had been victims of the system.
Whether well-intentioned or not,
somebody got the short shrift,
and they did,
and I started to
absorb a little guilt
and say, uh,
"I deserve,
I deserve it!"
I don't mean I deserve to get my house burned down.
The us
did
not in . . .
not,

I like to think, not intentionally,
but
maybe so,
there's just . . .
it's so
awful out there,
it was so *heart*breaking,
seeing those . . .
the devastation that went on
and people reduced to burning down their own
    neighborhoods.
Burning down our neighborhoods
I could see.
But burning down their own—
that was more dramatic
to me.

Kinda Lonely

The Park Family & Walter Park
Store owner, gunshot victim

(A very pleasant, sunny, high-ceilinged new modern home in Fullerton. There is a winding staircase that comes into a hallway. The furnishings are replicas of Louis XIV. Walter Park, who has had a gunshot through the eye, has a scar on the left side of his face. He is wearing a blue golf shirt, white socks and slippers, and khaki pants. His wife, June, is sitting on a love seat next to him. She is elegantly dressed. She has on a black silk blouse and yellow slacks and a wonderful concha belt with red stones. Chris Oh, her son and Walter's stepson, is in another chair, perpendicular to them. He is dressed simply and in his stocking feet. Birds and a lawn mower are very present throughout. The lawn mower moves close and then distant and then close. The birds are really beautiful. Piano music of Ravel's "Death of the Princess" playing on an excellent sound system.

(The feel of the place is airy but there is a lot of furniture. The love seat is in a sitting area with a sofa and two chairs and a marble table. There is a wooden cart with wheels and porcelain pitcher. The dining room has a cabinet with many porcelain items. Along the wall of the staircase is a long strip of fabric, which is a Korean banner. There is a tree which is real, in the living room, but other plants are silk or artificial. There is a painting of a white woman with a white baby at her breast. I think it was a rendering of Christ and Mary. It's clear that good taste and a lot of thought and joy went into the design. At the same time, it is clear it's an imitation of the European aesthetic.

(Mr. Park speaks in the rhythm of a person who has full authority and ease, and a person who has all of the facts exactly straight. When he begins talking, his wife and son shake their heads to let me know that he doesn't know the answer to the question. He is sitting with his arms crossed and legs crossed, also in an easy but confident and authoritative position. From his body position and his rhythm you would think this was the most reasonable, sound response possible. It is, of course, emotionally sound, but there is a gap between the question and the answer. He is heavily sedated, and has been since he was shot.

(He starts by nodding.)

I felt kind of
lonely,
you know,
in the store,
so I said
well,
I might need go
travel somewhere,
y'know,
and I said
well, I'm gonna probably go see
my mom
or, you know,
somebody.
So I try to go to Korea.
Then I call a couple guys up
and, uh,
"I feel kinda lonely.
I wanna go Korea,
see if I can change, uh,
situation,"
and they didn't say nothing.
(*Very passionate, and amazed*)

(Birds and lawn mower closer)
it's
kinda, you know,
wondering thing,
and one guy happened to tell me,
"Why you wanna go Korea
for?
You just came out of
hospital."
You know,
that,
that makes me wonder too.
So I came home and
I told her about it
and
she didn't say nothing.
Uh,
it happens to . . .
(His voice is much fuller here)
among the Koreans,
among Orientals,
if they really love somebody or they really like somebody,
they try
hide certain things
for different manner,
and, uh,
I accepted it as different manner
that
that's the way she loves
me and it's fine
as long as I know

and I have way to pay her back
that makes it even.
And she didn't say nothing.

To Drive

Chris Oh Medical student, stepson of
Walter Park

Besides, you know, being his son,
I also said I'm a medical student
and
I'd like to know
what the prognosis is
and I'd like to know
what you've done.
And, um,
they didn't tell me anything
and so here you are
and he's in this condition.
You don't know that he's already had
a bifrontal
partial lobectomy.
It's,
well, the bullet
passed through his temple—
temple side here—
and it went through his left eye

and lodged
in his frontal lobe.
And, um,
the frontal lobe is . . .
In the past,
in the old days,
they did a lot of frontal lobectomies
when they just removed
that part of the brain for people who are very tense and,
yeah,
lobotomies.
That's where your higher learning skills are,
your impulsiveness,
your willingness to do things,
and your, um,
I guess
your basic character.
(Pause)
And, um,
you know what . . . when you have . . . when you think
     and remember how
things used to be
and you realize you can't do those things now,
you
look different,
and
you can't drive.
I know he wants to drive.

And in My Heart for Him

Mrs. June Park Wife of Walter
Park

(She cries sometimes as she speaks, a natural
flow.)

He came to United States
twenty-eight years
ago.
He was very high-educated
and also very nice person to the people.
And he has business about seven,
what ten years,
twenty years,
so he work very hard
and he so hard
and he also
donated a lot of money to the Compton area.
And he knows the City Council,
the policemen, they knows him.
Then why,
why he has to get shot?
You know,
I don't know why.
So really angry, you know.
Then I cry
most of my life,

this is the time I cry lot,
so
I go to the hospital and I stay with him.
Especially ICU room
is they don't allow the family to
stay there,
but the,
all the nurses know me,
and every time I go there I bring some nice doughnuts
to the nurses and doctors,
and they find out how much I love him.
So they just let me in
and stay with him all day long.
So I just feed him
and stay till eight o'clock
at the night,
and all day long,
and I spend all my time
and in my heart for him.

Execution Style
Chris Oh

When
he got shot,
I guess he

pressed on the accelerator
and he ran into a telephone pole,
and at that moment
there was an African-American lady
behind
in her car
and witnessed
when it happened
and it was an Afro-American who shot him.
A man.
From
what I gather,
from what I heard
and things.
The gunman,
when he was at the stoplight,
the gunman
came up to the car and broke
the driver's side window
and, uh,
it wasn't one of those distant shots it was a close-
    range,
almost execution style.

The Beverly Hills Hotel

Elaine Young Real estate agent

(Saturday, February 1993. A real estate office in the heart of Beverly Hills. She has been in real estate for many years. She sold Sharon Tate the house she was murdered in. Most of her clients are movie stars. She was married to Gig Young. Elaine is a victim of silicone. She had plastic surgery done on her face, to insert cheek implants, and it exploded. She has been written about in several magazines. She is dressed in a bright blue dress with studs and earrings shaped like stars. She has dyed blond hair. She is very outgoing. The phone rings constantly. When her friends call, she puts them on the speakerphone, and I hear the entire conversation.)

So the second day—
this is what got me in trouble on television and really made
   me feel
bad.
I had a date
and my date canceled.
Now, mind you, I'm only three weeks separated and didn't
   want to be
alone
and my date canceled.
So now comes Saturday.
I had another date
and I thought if I have to be alone—
'cause my housekeeper goes off for the weekend.
I couldn't get to my daughter.

Still the rioting was escalating and it was really bad.
There were alerts: "Don't leave your house."
And I had a date
and he lives about twenty minutes away in the Valley and
    they say,
"Don't drive freeway."
And I said, "Are you going to see me tonight? 'Cause I don't
    want to
be alone."
And he said, "Yes."
So he came to pick me up.
And he got there and I said, "Oh my God, where are we
    gonna go?
We can't eat anywhere. Everything is closed." And I said,
"Wait a minute. A hotel wouldn't be closed. They gotta be
    serving
food."
So I said, "Let's see if we can go to the Beverly Hills
    Hotel."
So we drove to the hotel, which was a couple of minutes
    from my
house,
and when I got there, much to my shock,
the whole town, picture-business people,
had decided to do the same thing.
Only, unbeknownst to me, they did
it the night before too.
So basically what happened the three or four days of the
    heavy rioting,
people were going to the hotel,
and I mean it was mobbed.

So we would stay there till three or four in the morning.
    Everybody was
talking and trying to forget
what was going on . . . the rioting . . . try to . . . they
    would talk about it until
they'd exhausted the subject.
It would start out horrible,
scared, and "What was going on?"
And "How could this happen in California?"
And "Oh my God, what's happened to our town?"
And "These poor people . . ." and, and, and totally down
    and down and
down.
And then there's so much you can say.
In life
once you've hit bottom, there's no way to go but up.
So once you've talked about the bad and the horrible, you
    can't talk
about it anymore.
So then you say, "Well, let me put this out of my mind for
    now and
go on."
So that was the mood at the Polo Lounge
after they talked about how bad it was
and maybe they'd come back after an hour
but then they tried to go on.
"Here we are
and we're still alive,"
and, you know,
"we hope there'll be people alive
when we come out,"

but basically,
they would come there every night.
And I finally went there for three nights
and stayed till two or three in the morning
so I wouldn't be alone.
I talked to a lot of people.
I just want to clarify one thing.
In no way do I want to give the idea that I accepted the riot
in any way as . . .
or can even joke about it, because . . .
I can't imagine anybody jokin' about it.
I mean, I'm too interested in people,
in social
milieus and attitudes,
and to joke . . .
I took this thing extremely seriously and, uh,
no, not joking, absolutely not,
no way.
But anyway.
So when they interviewed me with the closing of the Polo
    Lounge
I commented about how we all went there, huddled
    together,
how we were there till two or three in the morning.
And oh, they say,
"What does the Polo Lounge remind them of?"
I said, "I went there thirty-six years for lunch.
I was there every day. I wrote my book there."
Well . . . the book starts out: "As I drove my car to the
    Beverly Hills
Hotel . . ."

Everything I did was there.
People magazine interviewed me there.
I did all my interviews there.
Sometimes when I was exhausted
I'd check in there for the weekend.
When my daughter was little,
we'd pretend like we're going on a vacation,
pack, get into the car, and
drive two and a half minutes.
Pretend like we're going away for the weekend.
I work so hard,
I don't have time to take a vacation.
So I'd check in there,
for two days, just to chill out.
So I was talking about that.
And then I said,
"And during the riots."
'Cause it was so foremost on my mind.
And I was talking about how we were all there.
Some man wrote me a letter.
"To Mrs. Young.
You are really an asshole.
You take life so lightly.
I saw your interview on television.
As far as I'm concerned,
you're a dumb shit bimbo
talking about having fun during the riots at the Polo Lounge.
How stupid can you be.
You're an embarrassment."
I mean, oh my God, I'm reading this letter.
I got it three weeks ago.

That's when the Polo Lounge closed.
It was like
oh my God,
if he only left his number,
so I can call him and explain that in no way did I mean to
    be flippant
on television about the riots. So he thought I was being
    flippant.
It was like
people hanging out together,
like safety in numbers.
No one can hurt us at the Beverly Hills Hotel
'cause it was like a fortress.

I Was Scared
Anonymous Young Woman
Student, University of Southern California

(February. A rainstorm. Late afternoon, early evening. Dark out. Just before dinner. A sorority house
at the University of Southern California, which is a
very affluent university in the middle of South-Central. We are in a small room with Laura Ashley furnishings. Lamplight. While we are talking, someone
comes by ringing a dinner bell which is like a xylo-
phone.)

I was scared to death.
I've never felt as scared, as frightened, in my life.
Um,
and it was a different fear that I've ever felt.
I mean, I was really afraid.
At a certain point
it dawned on us that they might try to attack the row,
the sororities and the fraternities.
Because they did do that during the Watts riots.
And, um, they . . .
they went
into the house,
where they smashed the windows.
I don't know how we got this information but somebody
    knew that,
so that
spread in the house real fast,
and once we realized that,
we started packing.

We all packed a bag and we all had put on our tennis shoes.

This was late in the evening, and we all sat in our hallways
    upstairs,

very small hallways,

and we all said,

"Oh, if they come to the front door, this is what we're
    gonna do."

Many things I can tell you.

First of all, my parents were on their way,

to drive to California,

to take part in a caravan

in which they bring old cars,

old forties cars,

and a whole bunch of 'em, all their friends, a huge club.

They all drive their cars around the country.

My dad has an old car.

It's a '41 Cadillac.

I told 'em to turn around, go home.

I said, "Go home, Mom."

All I can think of . . . one bottle,

one shear from one bottle in my father's car,

he will die!

He will die.

He collects many cars,

he has about fifteen different kinds of cars.

This is his thing, this is what he does.

He's got Lincoln

Continentals

and different Town and Countries.

All forties.

His favorite is a '41 Cadillac.

And, um, so . . . he keeps them from five to ten years,
you know.
Depending on whether you can get a good value for 'em.
It's a business
as well as a hobby.
And so I don't specifically know what car he came out in.
But one of 'em.
And those are his pride
and joys.
They are perfect.
They are polished.
They are run perfect.
They are perfect.
All I can think of is a bottle gettin' anywhere near it.

The Unheard

Maxine Waters Congresswoman, 35th District

(This interview is from a speech that she gave at the First African Methodist Episcopal Church, just after Daryl Gates had resigned and soon after the upheaval. FAME is a center for political activity in LA. Many movie stars go there. On any Sunday you are sure to see Arsenio Hall and others. Barbra Streisand contributed money to the church after the unrest. It is a very colorful church, with an enormous mural and a huge choir with very exciting music. People line up to go in to the services the way they line up for the theater or a concert.

(Maxine Waters is a very elegant, confident congresswoman, with a big smile, a fierce bite, and a lot of guts. Her area is in South-Central. She is a brilliant orator. Her speech is punctuated by organ music and applause. Sometimes the audience goes absolutely wild.)

First
African
Methodist Episcopal Church.
You all here got it going on.
I didn't know this is what you did at twelve o'clock on
    Sunday.
Methodist,
Baptist,
Church of God and Christ all rolled into one.
There was an insurrection in this city before
and if I remember correctly
it was sparked by police brutality.

We had a Kerner Commission report.
It talked about what was wrong with our society.
It talked about institutionalized racism.
It talked about a lack of services,
lack of government responsive to the people.
Today, as we stand here in 1992,
if you go back and read the report
it seems as though we are talking about what that report
    cited
some twenty years ago still exists today.
Mr. President,
THEY'RE HUNGRY IN THE BRONX TONIGHT,
THEY'RE HUNGRY IN ATLANTA TONIGHT,
THEY'RE HUNGRY IN ST. LOUIS TONIGHT.
Mr. President,
our children's lives are at stake.
We want to deal with the young men who have been
    dropped off of
America's agenda.
Just hangin' out,
chillin',
nothin' to do,
nowhere to go.
They don't show up on anybody's statistics.
They're not in school,
they have never been employed,
they don't really live anywhere.
They move from grandmama
to mama to girlfriend.
They're on general relief and
they're sleepin' under bridges.

Mr. President,
Mr. Governor,
and anybody else who wants to listen:
Everybody in the street was not a thug
or a hood.
For politicians who think
everybody in the street
who committed a petty crime,
stealing some Pampers
for the baby,
a new pair of shoes . . .
We know you're not supposed to steal,
but the times are such,
the environment is such,
that good people reacted in strange ways. They are not all
    crooks and
criminals.
If they are,
Mr. President,
what about your violations?
Oh yes.
We're angry,
and yes,
this Rodney King incident.
The verdict.
Oh, it was more than a slap in the face.
It kind of reached in and grabbed you right here in the
    heart
and it pulled at you
and it hurts so bad.
They want me to march out into Watts,

as the black so-called leadership did in the sixties,
and say, "Cool it, baby,
cool it."
I am sorry.
I know how to talk to my people.
I know how to tell them not to put their lives at risk.
I know how to say don't put other people's lives at risk.
But, journalists,
don't you dare dictate to me
about what I'm supposed to say.
It's not nice to display anger.
I am angry.
It is all right to be angry.
It is unfortunate what people do when they are frustrated
    and angry.
The fact of the matter is,
whether we like it or not,
riot
is the voice of the unheard.

Washington
Maxine Waters Congresswoman,
35th District

(I am in her office in Los Angeles. It is during a rainstorm. Late afternoon. Winter 1993. We talk for about two hours. Her original office had been burned down during the unrest.)

Oh, Washington
is, um,
a place where
ritual and custom
does not allow them
to,
uh,
talk about things that
don't fit nicely into
the formula.
I mean, our leadership
is so far removed
from what really goes on in the world
they, um,
it's not enough to say they're insensitive
or they don't care.
They really
don't
know.
I mean, they really don't see it,
they really don't understand it,
they really don't see their lives in

relationship to
solving these kinds of problems.
Um,
not only did they not talk about it,
um,
I had to force myself
on them in every way
and I did.
I was outrageous
in things that I did. *(She laughs)*
When I heard about a meeting at the White House
to talk about a kind of urban package,
I could not believe
that they would attempt to even try to have this meeting
without involving,
if not me,
the chairman of the Congressional Black Caucus,
if not me,
John Lewis,
who's supposed to be part of the leadership,
he is a whip,
part of the leadership, right?
I heard about this meeting on television,
And when I checked in with the Speaker
I asked the Speaker if there was a meeting going on.
He said yes.
I said, "I was not invited."
Uh.
"Who was invited?"
He said, "It's the leadership.
I don't control the

White House invitations. The President does the inviting
and it's not up to me to decide who's in the meeting."
And I told him,
I said,
"Well,
uh,
what time is this meeting?"
He said, "Well, I'm on my way over there now."
And I said,
"Well, I'll meet you over there,
because," I said,
"I'm coming
over."
And I was *angry*
and I went out,
I caught a cab.
I drive
but I didn't drive because I didn't trust myself.
I was angry.
I caught a cab.
I told the cabdriver, I said,
"Take me to the White House."
I said, "Hurry, I'm late.
I have an appointment at the White House."
He kind of looked at me like,
"yeah, right."
He took me there.
I used my little card,
my little
congressional card,
to show to the gate guard.

They don't know if I'm supposed to
be in this meeting or not,
so I show them the card. They open the gate. I went down,
opened the door.
Some lady inside
said, "Oh my God, we weren't expecting you."
I said, "You better tell them I'm here."
And I saw this big guard come out
and I was thinkin' to myself:
If they try
and put me out . . .
I started to plan what I was gonna do to this guard,
where I was gonna kick him,
and he looked at me
and he walked past, he didn't do anything.
Someone came out and said, "Right this way,
Congresswoman."
I said, "Thank you."
And the young lady ushered me.
I said,
"Where is my seat?"
And people kind of looked at me
and I sat down
and everybody sat down
and when the President
came in
everybody stood
and the President looked around the room
and he looked.
When he saw me
he looked,

he had a kind of quiz
on his face,
but he was nice.
His cabinet was there.
And, oh,
Sullivan
from
Health and Human Services,
one other
black was there,
and he went around the room
and they started to talk about this bill
that was being proposed, the enterprise zone bill,
and after about five or six persons I said,
"Mr. President,
Hi. I'm here because I want to tell you about what I think is
      needed
to deal with the serious problem
of unemployment,
hopelessness, and despair
in these cities."
I said, "Los Angeles burned
but Los Angeles is but one
city
experiencing
this kind of hopelessness and despair,"
I said, "and we need a job
program
with stipends . . ."
I said, "These young people
really,

ya know,
are not in anybody's statistics
or data.
They've been dropped off of everybody's agenda.
They live
from grandmama to mama to girlfriend."
I said,
"We now got young people
who are twenty, twenty-one, twenty-two years old
who have never worked a day of their lives."
I said, "These are the young people in our streets
and they are angry
and they are frustrated."
I said, "Don't take my word for it.
Ask Jack Kemp.
He's in housing projects. Ask him
what's going on out there."
Jack Kemp goes, "That's not my
department.
That's better asked of Secretary
Lynn Martin."
Well,
Lynn Martin was not there, but
her representative
was there
and it turns out
that this was a black man who didn't look black at
all.
He looked at the President
and he said,
"Mr. President,

she's right."
Well, the President's back stiffened
and he didn't try and relate to that.
He picked up on a part where I had talked about
the Justice Department.
I also said
that all of this anger and despair
was
exacerbated by the
excessive use of force
by police departments,
that the Justice Department
has never ever used its power
to do anything about
excessive force in these cities,
and that, in addition
to
this,
dealing with this joblessness,
the Justice Department of the United States is
going to have to find a way to intervene in these cities when
these
police departments are out of control.
So when this gentleman
from the Department of Labor supported
what I was saying and looked at the President
and said,
"This country is falling
apart."

Trophies

Paul Parker Chairperson, Free the LA
Four Plus Defense Committee

(Afternoon, October 1993. His girlfriend's house in
Westwood. He is dressed in Ivy League clothing. I
had seen him in court several times, where he wore
African clothing. He told me he wore Ivy League
clothing in Westwood, so as to be able to move
with the "program" and not to attract too much attention.)

So it's just a PR type of program.
Gates knew that the police were catching a lot of flak
and he
also caught a lot of flak from being at a benefit
banquet,
um, the time when the rebellion
was comin' down,
jumpin' off.
It just goes to show more or less the extremes that he went
    to just to
get these brothers.
And when they came for my brother Lance more or
    less,
they sent out two SWAT teams simultaneously,
one to my brother's and my fiancée's residence and one to
    my mom's.
They basically had *America's Most Wanted* TV cameras
    there.
Saying he was a known gang member,

a big head honcho drug dealer in the underground world for
   the last
two years,
he owns two houses,
things of this nature,
and here my brother went to college for four years,
he's been working in a law firm as a process server.
They basically paraded him around in the media,
saying we got the gunman, we got this guy.
They accused him of attempted murder, of shootin' at
   Reginald Denny,
um, with a shotgun. They said he
attempted to blow up some gas pumps
and my father got shot in the streets eleven years ago
over a petty robbery,
and Van de Kamp,
their attitude was "We don't want to bring your family
   through the
trauma and drama,
just stir up some more trouble."
They basically feel that if it's a black-on-black crime,
if it's a nigger killin' a nigger,
they don't have no problem with that.
But let it be a white victim,
oh,
they gonna . . . they gonna go
to any extremes necessary
to basically convict some black people.
So that's more or less how . . .
really what made me bitter
and I said well, I ain't gonna stand for this,

I'm not gonna let you
just put my brother's face around world TV headline news,
CNN world span,
and just basically portray him as a negative person.
I'm not gonna let you do that.
So that's more or less when I just resigned from my job,
more or less quit my job, and I just took it on.
And like I said, I been in law enforcement for a while, I
    been in the
army for six years,
I been doin' a lot of things.
So I just decided I'm not gonna let my brother, my one and
    only
brother, go down like that, my one and only brother,
my younger brother, so I decided to take this on full-time
and I was voted in as being chairperson of the Free the LA
    Four
Plus Defense Committee
and I been workin' for all the brothers ever since.
Because Denny is white,
that's the bottom line.
If Denny was Latino,
Indian, or black,
they wouldn't give a damn,
they would not give a damn.
Because
many people got beat,
but you didn't hear about the Lopezes or the Vaccas
or the, uh, Quintanas
or the, uh,
Tarvins.

You didn't hear about them,
but you heard about the Reginald Denny beating,
the Reginald Denny beating,
the Reginald Denny beating.
This one white boy
paraded all around
this nation
to go do every talk show there is,
get paid left and right.
Oh, Reginald Denny,
this innocent white man.
But you didn't hear nothin' about all these other victims
until the day of the trial came.
(*mimicking dorky voice*)
"Well, this is more than about Reginald Denny. This is
    about several
people. Many people got beat up on the corner."
So the bottom line is it, it, it's
a white victim, you know, beaten down by some blacks.
"Innocent."
I don't see it on the innocent tip,
because if that's the case,
then we supposed to have some empathy
or some sympathy toward this one white man?
It's like well, how 'bout the empathy and the sympathy
toward blacks?
You know, like I said before, we innocent. Like I said,
you kidnapped us,
you raped our women,
you pull us over daily,
have us get out of our cars, sit down on the curb,

you go through our cars,
you say all right,
take all our papers out, go through our trunk,
all right,
and drive off,
don't even give us a ticket.
You know we innocent,
you know where's our justice,
where's our self-respect,
but, hey, you want us to feel something toward
this white man, this white boy.
I'm like please,
it ain't happenin' here,
not from the real brothers and sisters.
That white man,
some feel that white boy just better be glad he's alive,
'cause a lot of us didn't make it.
They caught it on video.
Some brothers beatin' the shit out of a white man.
And they were going to do everything in their power to
    convict these
brothers.
We spoke out on April 29.
Hoo (*real pleasure*),
it was flavorful,
it was juicy.
It was, uh,
it was good for the soul,
it was rejuven . . .
it was . . .
(*count four, he sighs*)

it, it, it was beautiful.
I was a cornerback
and I ran some track
and played football,
everything.
I been all off into sports since I was five.
It was . . .
it was bigger than any . . . any type of win I've been
    involved in.
I mean, we been National Champions,
Golden State League.
I been . . .
I have so many awards and trophies,
but, um, it's . . . it's nothing compared to this.
They lost seven hundred million dollars.
I mean, basically you puttin' a race of people on notice.
We didn't get to Beverly Hills but
that doesn't mean we won't get there,
you keep it up.
Um,
they're talkin' about "You burned down your own
    neighborhoods."
And I say, "First of all,
we burned down these Koreans in this neighborhood."
About ninety-eight percent of the stores that got burned
    down were
Korean.
The Koreans was like the Jews in the day
and we put them in check.
You know, we got rid of all these Korean stores over here.
All these little liquor stores.

You know, we got rid of all that.
We did more in three days than all these
politicians been doin' for years.
We just spoke out.
We didn't have a plan.
We just acted and we acted in a way that was just.
Now we got some weapons, we got our pride.
We holdin' our heads up and our chest out.
We like yeah, brother, we did this!
We got the gang truce jumpin' off.
Basically it's
that you as black people ain't takin' this shit no more.
Even back in slavery.
'Cause I saw *Roots* when I was young.
My dad made sure. He sat us down
in front of that TV
when *Roots* came on,
so it's embedded in me
since then.
And just to see that aye aye.
This is for Kunta.
This is for Kizzy.
This is for Chicken George.
I mean,
it was that type of thing,
it was some victory.
I mean, it was burnin' everywhere.
It was takin' things and nobody was tellin' nobody.
It wasn't callin' 911.
"Aww they are takin'."
Unh-unh, it was like "Baby, go get me some too."

"I'm a little bit too old to move but get me somethin'."
You know, I mean, it was the spirit. I mean, actually today
they don't know who . . . who . . . who . . .
You know, they only got these . . .
What?
Eight people.
Eight people
out of several thousand?
Um *(real mock disappointment)*.
Um, um,
they lost.
Oh.
Big time.
No Justice No Peace.
That's just more or less, I guess you could say, motto.
When I finally get my house I'm gonna have just one room
    set aside.
It's gonna be my No Justice No Peace room.
Gonna have up on the wall No Justice,
over here No Peace,
and have all my articles
and clippings and, um,
everything else.
I guess so my son can see,
my children can grow up with it.
Know what Daddy did.
You know, if I still happen to be here,
God willin',
they can just see what it takes
to be a strong black man,
what you gotta do for your people,

you know.
When God calls you, this is what you gotta do.
You either stand
or you fall.
You either be black
or you die
and *(exhale)*,
you know, with No Justice No Peace
it . . . it's,
you know, um,
I guess you might say it's fairly simple,
but to me it's pretty, um,
not complex,
but then again it's deep,
it's nothin' shallow.
It basically just means if there's no justice here
then we not gonna give them any peace.
You know, we don't have any peace.
They not gonna have no peace,
a peace of mind,
you know,
a physical peace,
you know, body.
You might have a dent . . . a dent in your head from now
    on in life.
It might not be you
but it may be your daughter.
You know, somewhere
in your family
you won't have no peace.
You know, it . . . it's that type of thing.

178 **Anna Deavere Smith**

Without doing, say, justice,
if I don't do what I'm doing,
when I do
happen to die,
pass away,
I won't be able to really rest,
I won't have no peace,
'cause I didn't do something in terms of justice.
I'm one brother
doing the work of
one brother
and
I just do that,
the best that I can do.
It's educational.
It's a blessing.
It's a gift from God.

It's Awful Hard to Break Away

Daryl Gates Former chief of Los Angeles Police Department and current talk show host

(In a lounge at the radio station where he does a talk show. He is in great physical shape and is wearing a tight-fitting golf shirt and jeans. There is the sound of a Xerox machine. This is my second interview with him.)

First of all, I . . . I don't think it was a fund-raiser.
I don't think it was a fund-raiser at all.
It was a group of
people
who were in opposition
to Proposition F.
We're talking about long-term support.
We're talking about people who
came out and supported me right from the beginning
of this controversy,
when people were trying to get me to retire and everything.
Real strong supporters
of mine
and they were supporting
a no against Prop . . .
Proposition F.
And they begged me to be there
and I said I would and this is before we knew the . . . the,

uh, verdicts were coming in
and I didn't wanna go.
I didn't like those things, I don't like them at all,
but
strong supporters and I said I'll drop by for a little while,
I'll drop by,
and, um, so I had a commitment
and I'm a person who tries very hard to keep commitments
and somewhere along the way
better sense
should have
prevailed.
Not because it would have changed
the course of . . . of events in any way, shape, or form, it
    wouldn't have.
I was in constant contact with my office.
I have radio beepers, telephones,
uh,
a portable telephone . . .
telephone in my car,
just about everything you'd need
to communicate anywhere within our power.
But somewhere along the line
I should have said
my commitment to them is
not as important as my overall commitment to the . . . to
    the city.
When I . . . when I thought things were getting
to the point that I had . . . we were having some serious
    problems,
I was almost there.

My intent was to drop in say, "Hey,
I think we got a . . . a, uh,
riot blossoming.
I can't stay. I gotta get out of here."
And that's basically what I did.
The problem was
I was further away.
I thought it was in Bel Air. It turned out to be Pacific
    Palisades.
And my driver kept saying,
"We're almost there, we're almost there."
You know, he was kinda . . .
he wasn't sure of the distance either.
"We're almost there, Chief, we're almost there."
My intent was
to say, "Hey, I . . . I gotta get outta here," say hi,
and that's what I intended to do,
and it's awful hard to
break away.
I kept walking toward the door, walking toward the door.
People want a picture.
Shake your hand.
And it took longer than I thought it was
and I've criticized myself
from the very beginning. I've never, uh, I've never, uh,
justified that in any way, shape, or form.
I said it was wrong. I shouldn't have . . . I should have
    turned around.
I know better.
Would it have made any difference

if I had closeted myself in . . . in my office and did
    nothing?
I never would have been criticized.
But the very fact
that it gave that . . . that
perception of a fund-raiser,
and I know
in the minds of some
that's a big
cocktail party
and
it wasn't that at all, eh,
but, eh, in somebody's home
and there weren't that many people there at all
and anyway . . .
But I shouldn't have gone!
If for no other reason
than it's given
so many people
who wanted it
an opportunity to carp
and to criticize,
for . . . for
I should have been smarter.
I'm usually smart enough to realize hey,
I know I'll be criticized for that,
and I'm not going to give them the opportunity.
But for some
reason I didn't and, uh . . .
I think a lot of people who have . . . have
looked at me as being, uh,

stubborn and

obstinate

because I wouldn't compromise

and I was not going to be forced out of the department

and I believed it would be overall harmful to the
    department to be

forced out

and I think

the department was demoralized anyway

and I think it would just have absolutely

totally demoralized 'em.

And when I stood up,

they said, "Hey,

by golly, uh,

uh,

he's saying a lot of things that

I'd like to say."

And some of them were just shaking with anger because
    they were

being accused of things

that

they wouldn't think of doing and

didn't do

and they know the people around them,

their partners, wouldn't have done those types of things.

I don't think there's anyone who doesn't feel and isn't
    sensitive to

what is being said about them

day in and day out.

All you gotta do is pick up a newspaper and see what's
    being said

about you in the Los Angeles *Times*
and the . . . and, and the . . . and in the electronic media.
I mean, it was day in and day out.
Editorials
and all kinds of things.
I mean, the community activists
and most of them were really nasty
politicians,
nasty. I mean, they weren't so . . .
Nobody likes to read those types of things and more
     importantly
no one wants their friends and family
to read those kinds of things and I mean, uh, uh, it's a
     terribly difficult
thing to endure
and when people hear it over and over and over again.
And I make speeches
on college campuses all across the country
and I swear
I have a group,
mostly African-Americans,
and I swear
I am the symbol
of police oppression
in the United States,
if not the world.
I am.
Me!
And I ask them:
Who told you this?
What gave you this idea?

You don't know me.
You don't have any idea
what I've done.
Forty-three years in law enforcement,
no one has said that about me,
no one.
And suddenly
I am the symbol
of police oppression
and it's a tough thing to deal with,
a very tough thing.
You know,
just prior
to this,
in a poll
taken by a legitimate pollster,
the individual
with the greatest credibility
in the state of California—
I can't say the state
of California,
but the southern
part of the state of California—
was me.
The most popular Republican in Los Angeles
and Los Angeles County
was me.
I got more support
than
Ronald Reagan,
George Deukmejian,

what other Republicans,
Pete Wilson.
I got more support,
and suddenly!
suddenly!
I am the symbol.
And, you know,
on the day
that the Rodney thing [sic],
thing
happened,
the
President of the United States
was declaring me a national hero
for the work that I had done
in drugs
and narcotics
and the work that I had done with kids
and a lot of those kids were black kids.
And suddenly,
suddenly,
I am the symbol
of police oppression.
Just because some officers
whacked Rodney King
out in Foothill Division
while I was in Washington, D.C.

Human Remains

Dean Gilmour Lieutenant, Los Angeles County Coroner

(Afternoon, his office. A middle-aged man. Glasses. Very friendly. Speaks slowly.)

I been working with a . . .
an attorney
who is trying to have a *(aye)*
young lady—
I think she's twenty-one years of age—
declared dead,
um *(a small suck like a soft "t")*,
down at Fifty-eighth and Vermont.
There was
a New Guys
appliance store
and apparently
there were some looters inside
and the place caught fire.
Two of the looters, uh, was this girl and her boyfriend,
fiancé.
Appar . . .
from what we understand,
there were four or five
other, uh,
people in the store at the time
and
the boyfriend's the only one that escaped.

They don't know what happened to the other three or four
    people
but they do know that, um,
uh . . .
Well (quickly),
the mother of the girl says
she hasn't heard from her since (singsong)
then.
There's no insurance policies.
There's no reason to believe
she didn't perish in that building.
The boyfriend says,
"I last saw her over my shoulder,
but because of the heat and the smoke and the fire
I didn't, uh,
you know, I couldn't help her"
(on an exhale, and therefore substantially increased volume,
like a
release).
So that was the best information
that we had out of all the buildings.
That there may be human remains
in there.
We searched that place
four times.
And the fire was so hot
the ruff [sic, meaning "roof"]
had totally collapsed.
Rubble was about like so . . .
We couldn't find any human remains
and we went in with our forensic

anthropologist
and her search teams.
We went in with, um *("t" sound),*
uhh,
uh, dogs,
search dogs that we brought in from Northern California.
We made four attempts, if I recall correctly.
We couldn't find a tooth
or a finger or anything.
The family doesn't have . . .
They can't really get on with their life until they have
    some
resolution to it
(a breath, covering a burp?).
And that's the thing about our society is *until,*
um,
until there's some type of a *service,*
whatever it is,
whether there's a cremation
or there's a burial,
uh,
most people just can't let go
with their lives
and then pick up the pieces and start
from there.
There has to be some resolution.
(Pause)
There were fifty-two deaths.
We were looking seriously at sixty
and again there wasn't a *whole*
lot of information.

Just because somebody died
during this time frame doesn't mean it was directly
    related
to the riot.
We were able to look at each individual death.
If we couldn't . . .
if we didn't have enough *facts* to . . . *to*
support it,
we would say no,
we can't definitely call this.
But again it wasn't just in South-Central.
We had one out in the Valley *(singsong)*.
We had one in Pasadena
where there was a party
and the
police arrived with a helicopter.
Seems to me it was Pasadena or
Altadena, up that way,
and
some of these . . . I think the party was being
    crashed
by gang members,
which brought up an interesting point.
Are all gang shootings during this time riot-related?
I mean, we have gang shootings every day
of the year.
What would set these apart from being riot-related?
And . . . and, as I recall, I think someone had shot at a
    police helicopter
and one of the people in the neighborhood,
in the block there,

was shot.

So that was one.

Now,

was this just a bunch of kids having a party

who got carried away

and somebody started shooting at the chopper

'cause they were drunk

or was it because of the riots?

What was interesting was one of the cases I was looking at
    was in

Hollingback Division.

Hollingback is East LA.

They didn't have *any* riot-related deaths

in East Los Angeles.

So,

um,

one guy was found, um, I can't remember if he was stabbed
    or shot

inside of a drainage pipe,

and they said no, it was definitely not riot-related.

I don't know whether it was a lovers' quarrel

or . . . or a bad dope deal

or what,

but they said it definitely didn't have anything to do with the
    riots,

it was just

another homicide.

Um, so that's how we ended up with sixty,

and oh,

I think it was by July

we were able to whittle the number

down to . . .
(a breath)
And since then we found some human remains
in some of the rubble,
several months later.
That was a riot building,
um,
and we were able to identify the person.
Human remains?
Human remains
is what we . . .
you and I leave behind.
We don't die like this necessarily.
Uh, we . . .
especially in a hot fire
you're charred.
You also, after the fact,
have animal activity.
Dogs
and . . . and other critters come along
and will disarticulate
bodies.
Uh,
rats,
uh,
all kinds of,
uh,
varmints and stuff.
And once we're gone
we . . . we don't take very good care of ourselves, you
know,

so . . .
We have the same thing out in the boonies,
up here in the mountains or out in the desert.
Skeletonized bodies
that have little teeth marks
where the rats
have started gnawing the bones,
because they go after the marrow and stuff.
You don't have an entire body necessarily.
If there's a tremendous explosion,
um . . .
Let me see if I have those numbers.
We published some numbers.
(He is going through his sheets of paper from now until nearly the
end of his talk, flipping over stapled sheets)
I can't see real well without my spectacles.
(He puts on his glasses)
See if I can find that press release.
See, the hardest part of this job is the families,
the survivors, um . . .
You know this person's
no longer in pain.
They no longer have to worry about
the April 15th deadline.
They don't have to worry about
paying their bills
or . . . or AIDS
or any of those other things that
those of us who are alive worry about.
But, um,

I've lost . . .
My first child was a full-term stillborn.
My brother was murdered up in Big Bear
and the guy got four years' probation.
Um,
my sister was killed by a drunk driver,
leaving three kids
and a husband
behind.
So I can empathize with these families as far as what they've gone
through.
(still turning pages, now just the sound of the pages)
Oh, here we go.
Forty-one gunshot wounds.
These are the races.
Okay, but these are not official.
Some of these are not.
Twenty-six black,
Eighteen Hispanic,
Ten Caucasian,
Two Asian.
Uh, types of death.
Gunshot wounds were forty.
Uh, traffics were six.
Four assaults,
Four arsons and four others.
Sex were fifty-one males
and seven females.
Um,
there were seven officer-involved fatalities.

Four involved LAPD,
One with sheriff,
One with Compton,
One with the National Guard.
So . . .
Let's pray for peace, hunh?

(Abrupt blackout)

(Here there should be a musical cue)

Scenes from the Disturbances

©1992, Los Angeles Times/Kirk McKoy

©1992, Los Angeles Times/Kirk

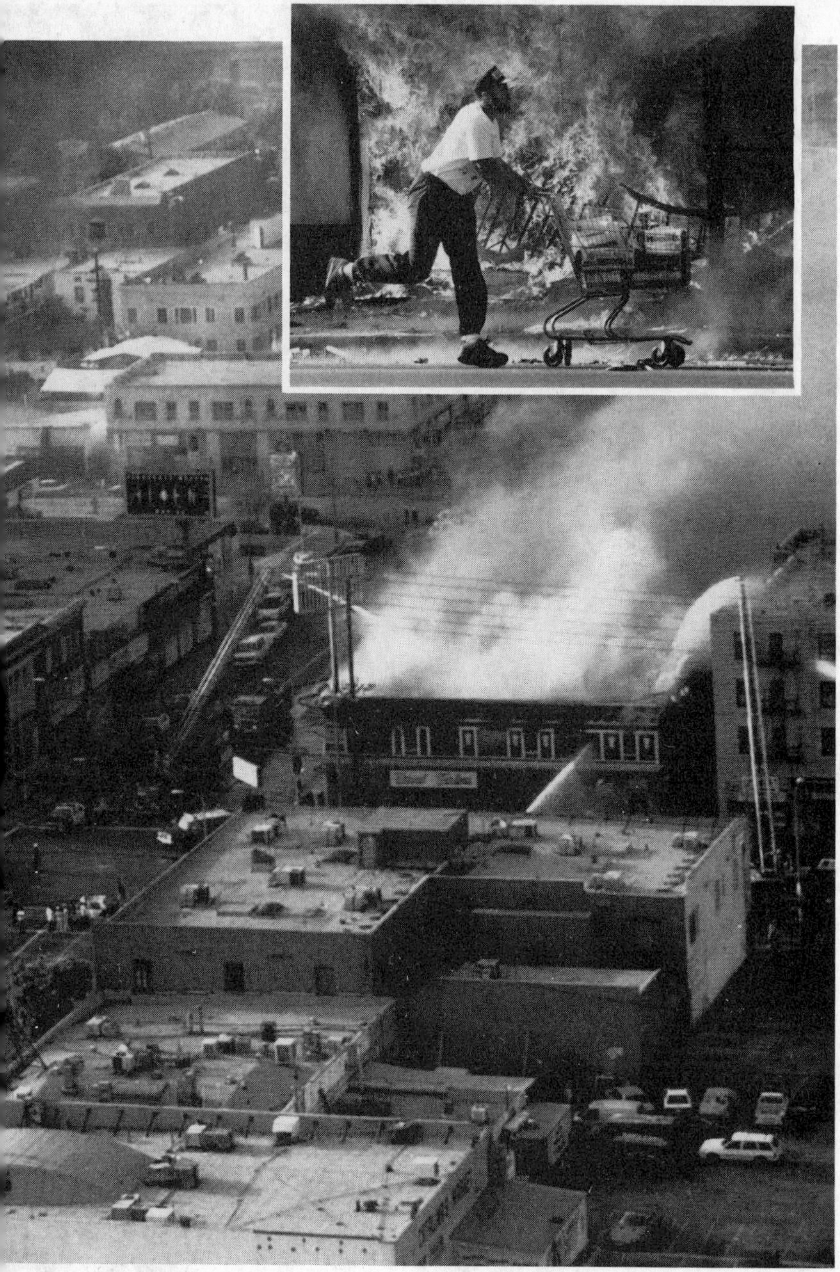

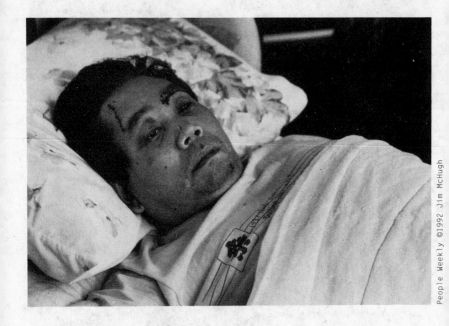

Twilight

Long Day's Journey into Night

Peter Sellars Director, Los Angeles Festival

(Sunday morning, February 1993. We are at the Pacific Dining Car restaurant. Peter tells me it's a place where power breakfasts happen. There are very few people there. It's an old-fashioned kind of restaurant. Peter gets very emotional while he speaks, almost in tears.)

Dad . . . he won't replace the burnt-out light bulbs.
You know, he yells at the family for complaining and
    condemns everyone
to live in darkness.
'Cause he's too cheap
to put in some light bulbs.
That's what America feels like right now.
Just asked him for some light bulbs.
Burned out here and here and here.
Couldn't we replace them?
With brighter ones?
And . . . James Tyrone . . .
he's too cheap.
He rants on and on about everything he's always done for
    you.
How he's lived his whole life just to support his family.
But he won't replace the light bulbs.
And he's grew up on a culture of success.

So the only thing that was of any interest to this man has to be
success,
you know,
which is America.
Here's a man who has been a success
and of course he's at home with that.
Right now in America, there isn't a family . . .
We may have a good GNP
but not a family to come home to.
Can't live in our own house.
That's what the LA riots is about.
We can't live,
our own house burning.
This isn't somebody else's house,
it's our own house.
This is the city we are living in.
It's our house.
We all live in the same house . . .
Right, start a fire in the basement
and, you know,
nobody's gonna be left on the top floor.
It's one house.
And shutting the door in your room,
it doesn't matter.
Fact is, you have a stronger sense of getting
     incinerated,
you know, and the task is,
you know.
I mean, Eugene O'Neill
wrote the classic play about
the American dream.

I Remember Going. . .

Rev. Tom Choi Minister, Westwood
Presbyterian Church

(In a pastor's office in the church, a church with an
affluent congregation. Afternoon, during a rainstorm, winter 1993. He is a tall, slender Chinese-
American man. He was educated at Yale Divinity
School and labors during the interview to be clear
and not to overstate.)

I remember going out
finally on Saturday to, um, do some cleanup work.
And I remember
very distinctly
going down there and choosing to wear my clerical collar.
And I haven't worn my clerical collar for about seven or
     eight years,
you know,
because, you know, people call me "Father,"
all this kind of stuff,
and I didn't like that identification.
But I remember doing that specifically
because I was afraid that somebody
would mistake me for a Korean shop owner
and . . . and, um, either berate me physically or beat me
     up.
So I remember hiding behind this collar
for protection.
The reason why a minister should wear a collar
is to proclaim . . .

to let everybody know who he is and what he is,
but I'm using it for protection,
which I, I knew about that
and I said, "Gee."
But I didn't take it off.
Anyway, I went down
and we were asked to go
and pick up
stuff from the Price Club
and so I had to go down to the bank
and get money
and I went to the area.
Also I remember some people complaining
that Korean-Americans didn't patronize black businesses.
So I made sure that I went to black businesses for lunch
and whatnot, wearing my collar and waiting around for food.
And I remember just going to people and people just
      looking at me.
And . . . and I usually kind of slump over when I walk, but
      in this case I
kind of stood straight and I had my neck high
and I made sure that everyone saw my collar.
(Laughs)
And . . . and I, I just went to somebody and, um, who was
      standing
next in line and I said,
"How are you doing?"
Every . . . every place I went
I got the same answer:
"Oh, I'm doing all right.
How are you?"

And I said, "Oh, I'm just trying to make it."
And there'd be a chuckle.
And . . . and agreement.
And then we just started having this conversation.
And in every instance,
you know,
of these people that quote unquote
were supposed to be hostile on TV and whatnot,
there was nothing but warmth,
nothing but a sense of . . . of
"Yeah, we should stick together" and nothing but friendliness
that I have felt,
and this was, um, a discovery
that I had been out of touch with this part of the city.
After a couple of days
I stopped wearing the collar
and I realize that if there's any protection I needed
it was just whatever love I had in my heart to share with
    people that
proved to be enough,
the love that God has taught me to share.
That is what came out in the end for me.

A Jungian Collective Unconscious

Paula Weinstein Movie producer

(On the phone. About 11 P.M. Chicago time. She is at the Four Seasons Hotel in Chicago. She has been on a movie set all day, shooting on location.)

You know it was odd, we felt—
Mark and I think—slightly isolated in our world
that was seeing it as a riot and an uprising.
There's both horror and rage and a sense of extreme
    impotence,
and saying, "What are we gonna do?"
So,
I got together with a group of people
and we organized a press conference on
the Warner Brothers lot
on
Wednesday,
um,
with
the entertainment industry people,
and it was
really quite an extraordinary event
because
some people objected,
even as late as Wednesday,
to the fact that our press release
said . . .

calling it an uprising
and decrying the verdict.
And
some
powerful people in Hollywood
called up, having looked at our press release,
and saying,
"Well we agree with everything but how can you decry the
    verdict?"
(She laughs)
And we said, You can't, you know.
This is not gonna happen
if people in the entertainment industry are gonna get up and
    speak
out.
The truths gotta be told.
We're not gonna, like,
pretend to be parents here,
and it was such an obvious
paternalistic
response.
And there was a lot of
discomfort,
I felt,
not amongst the young actors,
not amongst
some of the young directors,
but amongst the older
group,
that were more established,
that there should be

a response saying,
"Stop the violence."
But not one that was prepared to say,
"This verdict is out of the question
and we don't blame you."
And it was a funny thing
because
we did this press conference on
twenty-four-hour notice,
again
because Hollywood is a little bit about putting on a show.
People were worried and saying,
"Gee, what happens if the news media don't show up,
or the wrong people show up and you *fail*?"
There is a sense
of, "If we're going to go out
we have to make sure that we don't fail,"
which has come from
twenty years of Republican and
Democratic
party politics—
as opposed to street politics—
where it isn't about failing,
it's about
struggle
and telling the truth
and being angry
and
so what if only three people show up?
You've done something.
And then there was . . .

Our house became,
it was,
there were about fourteen kids
who live in West Hollywood
and
who work at Warner Brothers or at our company
who came
to live at our house.
Well, they feel like kids—
early twenties
to mid twenties—
and they all moved in
because they felt their houses weren't safe.
Yeah,
their houses weren't safe.
And they had come to our company
because of our politics
and known it was a place to come and talk,
so we said come back to our house and stay with us,
and
it became
Camp Rosenberg for the next five days.
(she listens)
In Brentwood,
I think was the most interesting thing for me,
which was taking
all these kids
who'd grown up
hearing about the sixties,
who were political,
who had no place to put it—

white kids,
black middle-class kids
who were living at our house—
and for them,
being glued to the television,
they had a kind of Jungian collective unconscious
connection,
as political kids,
now, with what happened before,
but no place to put it.
I was organizing this press conference and on the phone all
    night
going down with the food.
I'm sure you've heard from everybody what those weeks
    were like.
People who had lived in Los Angeles all their lives,
had never been to South Central,
I mean, went in caravans with me.
I mean, that's pretty scary.
I don't know any other city that would happen in.
I'm in Chicago now,
people are in the South Side all the time,
you can't avoid it,
and everyone knows Harlem,
and it isn't true
in Los Angeles.
A lot of people who have lived there for twenty-five years
had never ever gone.
And these kids had never gone.
It's as if it is a different
country,

and that's the view—
and that's the horror of Los Angeles.
So it was an extraordinary time.
First I went to the AME,
and from there I went to Diane Watson's headquarters,
and
first we went
throughout Beverly Hills and West L.A.
and made everybody give us food
and talk about feeling like I was back in SDS,
trashing someplace,
going in and saying you've got to give us food
and stopping everybody who was on the line out
for money
and everybody on every aisle—
"Give me a buck, give me this"—
and watching their reactions to it
was also fabulous for these kids.
It was like street theater.
There they were going up
to managers—
they watched
me do it a couple of times—
and going up to the people and organizing
people in Mrs. Gooch's in Beverly Hills,
and at one point we had run out of stuff
and we kept going down,
and in the early—
in the morning, when we went,
it was . . .
there were lots of people in clean-up and all of that

by
late
Saturday afternoon.
You got there
and
and the line
of people distributing food
into Diane Watson's,
right behind her headquarters,
into the warehouse there,
was now a completely
multiracial
and multicultural line of people.
Young people in their twenties
passing food
and everybody . . .
everytime someone came up
in a Mercedes or a station wagon or whatever
with food, who had never been there before,
everybody was applauding,
and there was a sense
of
a community here,
and you
felt the possibility,
you believed
that it actually could change,
and of course
here we are a year later,
(seven-second pause)
didn't change.
All,

all
the
language
was there,
and all the big gestures
were there,
and,
and,
I guess
what disturbed me,
which I really . . . what I would wanna talk about the most
about that week,
was watching rich white people guard
their houses
and send their children
out of L.A.
as if
the devil was coming after them.
And
it wasn't realistic.
It was,
I think, a media fest
of making white people
scared
of the African-American community,
and, and
nothing had changed.
Nothing.
And everybody—
people who were well-intentioned and understood that
    nothing had
changed . . .

The degree to which
the city—
the white community—
went into a sense of real terror,
and, and
an inward looking self-protectiveness,
as opposed to standing up and saying,
"We are gonna stand by whatever,
if the verdict is this,
and
these people are found not guilty,
it will be unjust and we will stand together."
It was as if nothing,
no connection, had been made,
because it can't be made
in four days.
It's a fake . . .
It was a fake
euphoria we all felt.
It was the euphoria of,
"Look at what's possible not what's real."
Uhm,
and, and
everything
retreated,
and the most—
the heightened example of it being retreated was . . .
of the retreating was the way
the media treated
the last week
and the way

the white community reacted to it
and the rich white community reacted to it.
(five-second pause)
(much lower volume, much less intention)
Everybody's scared in L.A.

Application of the Laws

Bill Bradley Senator, D-New Jersey

(His office in the Senate Building. A Sunday in February 1993. A well-lit office with wonderful art on the wall. He is dressed in jeans but is wearing very elegant English shoes. His daughter is in the other part of the empty office doing her homework. They are on their way to a basketball practice for her.)

I mean, you know, it's still . . .
there are people who are, uh,
who the law treats in different ways.
I mean, you know, one of the things that strike me about,
uh, the events of Los Angeles, for example, was, um, the
    following:
I have a friend,
an African-American,
uh, was, uhhh,
I think a second-year Harvard Law School student.
And he was interning
a summer in the late seventies
out in LA, at a big law firm,
and every Sunday
the . . . the different partners would . . .
would invite the interns to their home
for tea or brunch or whatever.
And this was a particular Sunday and he was on his way
    driving
to one of the partners' homes.

There's a white woman in the car with him.
I think she was an intern.
I'm not positive of that.
They were driving and they were in the very . . .
just about the neighborhood of the,
uh, partner, obviously well-to-do neighborhood in Los
    Angeles.
Suddenly he looks in the rearview mirror.
There is a, uh, police car,
red light.
He pulls over.
Police car pulls in front of him,
pull . . . police car pulls behind him,
police car pulls beside of him.
Police jump out,
guns, pull him out of the car,
throw him to the floor,
put a handcuff on him behind his back.
All the while pointing a gun at him.
Run around to the woman on the other side. "You're being
    held
against your will, aren't you, being held against your will."
She gets hysterical
and they keep their guns pointed.
Takes them fifteen or twenty minutes to convince them.
"No, no, I'm not, uh, I'm not, uh, I'm, I'm, I'm, I'm an
    intern, law firm,
I'm on my way to a meeting, partner's brunch."
And after that, he convinces them of that, while his head is
    down in
the ground, right?

They take the handcuff off.

They say, "Okay, go ahead."

They put their hats on, flip their sunglasses down, get in
    their police

cars, and drive away, as if nothing happened.

So my first reaction

to that is, um . . .

The events of April aren't new

or the Rodney King

episode isn't news in Los Angeles

or in many other places.

My second thought is: What did the partner of that law firm
    do on

Monday?

Did the partner call the police commissioner?

Did the partner call anybody?

The answer is no.

And it gets to, well,

who's got responsibility here?

I mean, all of us have responsibility

to try to improve the circumstances

among the races of this country.

I mean, you know, uh, a teenage mother's got a
    responsibility

to realize that if she has more children the life chances of
    those

children are gonna be less;

the gang member's gotta be held accountable for his finger
    on a gun.

Right?

The corporate executive has gotta be responsible for hiring and
promoting diverse talent
and the head of the law firms gotta be responsible for that as well,
but
both the corporate executive and the law firm have to use their moral power.
It's not a total contradiction.
I don't think it is. The moral power of the law firm
or corporation when
moments arise such as my friend's face in the ground with the gun
pointed at his head because he was in the wrong neighborhood and
black
and the moral power of those institutions have to be brought to bear
in the public institutions, which in many places are not
fair.
To put it mildly.
Right? And the application of the law
before which we are all in *theory* equal.

Something Cooking Here

Otis Chandler A director of the
Times Mirror Company

(Former editor of the Los Angeles *Times*. An
elegant man, thoughtful and soft-spoken. We are
in an office at the *Times*. He is drinking iced
tea.)

I think
if you think about America and you think about the
    families
that have had the opportunities
by accumulation of wealth, whether it be newspapers or
    mining
or
whatever, and you think about
who . . . what families
have really made a contribution over many generations,
    there aren't
many.
I can think of the
(*He counts his fingers*)
Kennedys,
the Rockefellers,
maybe the Mellons in Pittsburgh,
hopefully,
immodestly, the Chandlers
in Los Angeles,

but there aren't very many.
Most of 'em
just sat around and piddled the wealth away,
became alcoholics or whatever. They couldn't . . . couldn't
    take the
notoriety
and the open door.
They didn't go for it.
But
I don't want you to go away
from this
visit thinking that I'm . . .
that I
feel it's hopeless
or that it can never be made right
or that we should just throw money at it
or we should just make speeches.
It's going to have to be a lot of things
and a lot of people participating,
but there has to be that commitment
for the long term.
It can't be
well, let's just
do a couple things
for a few years and it will go away.
I think, Anna,
we're talking about
a long time
to get a handle on this.
We're talking about a lot of things
that are gonna be tried

and fail.
We're going to have to be patient,
we're going to have to be resolute,
that this is all going to . . . someday,
whether
it's five years or ten years,
but this is going to be a safe,
pleasant city
for everybody,
regardless of where they live
or what they do
or what the color of their skin is.
Somehow we have to make
that wonderful . . .
Somehow we have to make
that dream
come true
and I'm not going to give up.
Somehow this whole thing cannot be allowed to lapse
back into business as usual.
There's nothing to stop . . .
within another year or two . . .
I wish I could answer your question
and provide hope.
There's hope but there's no easy answer.
I've thought a lot about that
and I'll give you a few thoughts.
We mustn't . . .
we,
the whole community,
political leadership,

private leadership,
we can't allow
again
the situation to be . . .
to deteriorate
again
after a year or two years of hope and building
and new alliances, promises,
political speeches,
a new mayor, all of the things that are going on now,
and then
be diverted.
Inevitably
other things creep on the agenda
and pretty soon,
human nature being what it is,
and
that
can't happen again
because it happened before.
That's what I'm telling you.
It happened before.
There was just as much commitment,
there was just as much passion
and violence and hate.
See, after the Watts riots there was something called the
    McClellan
Commission.
Fine.
That was for two years
and we forgot about Watts.

So here we are again.
We all have to make a commitment
that this is never going to happen again
to Los Angeles,
and we have to meet
on a regular basis,
and we have to have the
power
in this group,
quasi-public
quasi-
political group,
that we can call the governor,
that we can call the publisher of the LA *Times*,
the President of the United States,
and say,
"hey,
we gotta see you,
we got something
cookin here."
It's gonna cost all kinds of money.
(four counts of pause)
I think businesses should give some,
government should give some,
and I think we're gonna have to be taxed.
Hit us all on
sales tax
or gasoline tax
or something
and take a cent or two from everybody
and build up some kind of fund.

You got to have money.
And I realize what I'm gonna hear from people who want
    money for
education and AIDS and
health care. Those are very, very important.
This is more important to me,
'cause if our cities deteriorate into jungle land, which they are
    now . . .

A Deadeye

Owen Smet Culver City Police
Department, former range manager, Beverly
Hills Gun Club

(There are guns' shooting sounds in the background. He is wearing tinted glasses and a black
silk jacket.)

After the riots our business went up forty percent, maybe
     as much as
fifty percent.
We have a membership here that shoots,
riots or no riots,
but because of the feeling of
danger overall in the community . . .
Long time ago you used to say there's some areas of LA
     County
where you couldn't walk
after dark,
and it's progressed to the point where you say,
     "Gee,
there's no place
safe
in LA County, daylight *or* dark."
People are looking for an opportunity to defend
     themselves.
They just need something,
and this is one of the places they come.
Shooting is a skill just like anything else.

A deadeye?

Is a very good shot.

Yes,

I am a deadeye.

I'm not a natural one.

I spent

couple years in Vietnam,

and that will make you good if nothing else.

You don't want to get over there and hit your
   foot.

(*The shooting starts*)

Sure,

a lot of these are handguns.

If you look at the top row, those are the smaller-caliber
   guns,

twenty-twos,

and then as you work your way on down to the bottom
   row,

that's the forty-fives.

I guess you'd say the least powerful at the top

to the most powerful at the bottom.

Probably the most powerful here

are the forty-fives.

This is a forty-four

Magnum gun,

probably the most powerful handgun that we have
   here.

I usually start people with a thirty-eight.

One of the most popular for the drive-bys are the nine
   millimeters.

But the gang members and some of the more organized
     groups out
there are using everything,
everything.
There's no question about it, they
are probably better armed than we are.

Ask Saddam Hussein

Elaine Brown Former head of the
Black Panther Party, author, *A Taste of Power*

(A pretty black woman in her early fifties. She is in a
town outside of Paris, France, on the phone. It is 5
P.M. France time. Spring.)

I think people do have, uh,
some other image
of the Black Panther Party than the guns.
The young men, of course, are attracted
to the guns,
but what I tell them is this:
Did you know Jonathan Jackson?
Because I did,
and Jonathan Jackson was seventeen years old.
He was probably one of the most brilliant young men
that you could meet.
He happened to be a science genius.
He was not a gang member, by the way,
but Jonathan Jackson
went to a courtroom by himself
and took over for that one glorious minute
in the name of
revolution and the freedom of his brother
and other people who were in prison
and died that day.
My question to you,
seventeen-year-old young brother with a gun in your hand,

tough and strong and beautiful as you are:
Do you think it would be better
if Jonathan Jackson were alive today
or that he died
that day in Marin County?
Me personally,
I'd rather know Jonathan Jackson.
That's what I'd rather do,
and I'd rather him be alive today,
to be among the leadership that we do not have,
than to be dead and in his grave at seventeen years old.
I'm talking merely about strategy,
not swashbuckling.
I think that this idea of picking up the gun and going into
     the street
without a
plan and without
any more rhyme or reason than rage
is bizarre and so, uh . . .
And it's foolish
because it will, uh . . .
I think that
all one has to do
is ask, to ask the Vietnamese
or Saddam Hussein
about the power and weaponry
and the arsenal of the United States government and its
     willingness to
use it
to get to understanding what this is about.
You are not facing a,

you know, some little Nicaraguan clique
here.
You are not in Havana in 1950 something.
This is the United States of America.
There isn't another *country*,
there isn't another *community*
that is more organized and armed.
Uh,
not only is it naive,
it is foolish if one is talking
about jumping out into the street
and waving a gun,
because you not that bad,
you see what I'm saying?
You just not that bad.
You *think* you bad,
but I say again,
ask Saddam Hussein
about who is bad
and you'll get the answer.
So what I am saying is:
Be conscious of what you are doing.
If you just want to die
and become a poster,
go ahead and do that—
we will all put you on the wall with all the rest of the
    people.
But if you want to effect change for your people
and you are serious about it,
that doesn't mean throw down your gun.
Matter of fact, I would def . . . definitely never tell
    anybody to do that,

not black and in America.
But if you want a gun,
I hope you can shoot
and I hope you know who to shoot
and I hope you know how to not go to jail for having done
    that
and then let that be the end of that.
But if you are talking about a war
against the United States government,
then you better talk to Saddam Hussein
and you better talk to the Vietnamese people
and the Nicaraguans
and El Salvadorans
and people in South Africa
and people in other countries in Southeast Asia
and ask those motherfuckers
what this country is capable of doing.
So all I am saying is:
I'm saying that
if you are *committed,*
if you seriously make a *commitment,*
because . . .
and that commitment
must be based not on hate but on love.
And that's the other thing.
My theme is
that love of your people.
Then you gonna have to realize that this may have to be a
    lifetime
commitment
and that the longer you live,

the more you can do.
So don't get hung up
on your own ego
and your own image
and pumping up your muscles
and putting on a black beret
or some kinda Malcolm X hat or whatever other
regalia
and symbolic vestment you can put on your body.
Think in terms of what
are you going to do
for black people.
I'm saying that these
are the long haul,
because then you might be talkin' about
bein' in a better position for a so-called
armed struggle.
At this point you talkin' about a piss-poor,
ragtag, unorganized, poorly armed
and poorly, poorly,
uh-uhm,
poorly led
army
and we will be twenty more years
trying to figure out what happened to Martin, Malcolm,
and the Black Panther Party.

Twilight #1

Homi Bhabha Literary critic/
Writer/Scholar

(Phone interview. He was in England. I was in L.A.
He is part Persian, lived in India. Has a beautiful
British accent.)

This twilight moment
is an in-between moment.
It's the moment of dusk.
It's the moment of ambivalence
and ambiguity.
The inclarity,
the enigma,
the ambivalences,
in what happened in the L.A.
uprisings
are precisely what we want to get hold of.
It's exactly the moment
when the L.A. uprisings could be something
else
than it was
seen to be,
or maybe something
other than it was seen to be.
I think when we look at it in twilight
we learn
to . . .
we learn three things:

one, we learn that the hard outlines of what we see in
    daylight
that make it easy for us to order
daylight
disappear.
So we begin to see its boundaries in a much more faded
    way.
That fuzziness of twilight
allows us to see the intersections
of the event with a number of other things that daylight
    obscures for
us,
to use a paradox.
We have to interpret more in
twilight,
we have to make ourselves
part of the act,
we have to interpret,
we have to project more.
But also the thing itself
in twilight
challenges us
to
be aware
of how we are projecting onto the event itself.
We are part of
producing the event,
whereas, to use the daylight
metaphor,
there we somehow think
the event and its clarity

as it is presented to us,
and we have to just react to it.
Not that we're participating in its clarity:
it's more interpretive,
it's more creative.

Magic #2
Betye Saar Artist

(Phone interview. She lives in Laurel Canyon.)

It was, um,
still light,
because it didn't last for a very long time.
So it's like this sort of in between day and night
when the sky is sort of gray
and we were walking back to the car
and Tony, who was very political, was sort of adamant about
there was gonna be trouble and so forth
and we were making plans to go to dinner
and when we got to go to dinner, the area
we wanted, it was dark already
and we were going to a place up toward the moun . . .
up toward the Hollywood Hills
and we couldn't get by
because of people in the streets
and
disturbances.
Now, this is in West Hollywood,
where there was not . . .
where there is a predominantly
gay and lesbian population
and these were mostly gay men
who were
protesting the uprising by,
uh, writing "guilty" on the pos . . .

graffiti,
they were actually doing graffiti work,
and the street was actually blockaded,
they were protesting the verdict,
and we went to the restaurant and we heard
more protesting on the radio.
But to get back to the sky.
That's kind of what I remember about the sky,
the kind of surreal time of day,
because it's between day and night,
and I hadn't
heard anything else about the rest of the city
until I got home.
It's sort of limbo time,
and the same with dawn,
because it's not night or day,
because it's transition,
and to me it implies a sort of limbo.
It's very surreal, I think,
or maybe even magical.
But magic is not always good,
because it implies
all sorts of things,
like evil
and control.
I just use it like magical, like enchantment,
that sort of mystical quality,
and some people
think that it's the work of Satan and so forth.

Justice

Screw Through Your Chest

Harland W. Braun Counsel for
defendant Theodore Briseno

I didn't want to take the case
because I regard it as a racial beating
and my son had had a racial incident.
He is in Princeton.
My son was going to
Harvard boy's school over here in Coldwater.
He was driving over here
in Westwood.
He had a two-seater Mercedes
and he was the passenger
and his friend
was driving the car
and his friend's mother is a partner
at O'Melveney and Myers.
They're driving, I guess, a Tuesday or a Wednesday night
and LAPD pulls them over.
My son is sort of outspoken.
I don't know where he gets that from,
but
he
jumps out of the car
and says to the cop,
"I know why you stopped us—

because Bobby's Black."
Which is obviously true.
I mean, Westwood,
Mercedes,
a Black kid driving a Mercedes.
They thought he was a dope dealer or something.
They're gonna pull him over.
So the cop turns to my son and says,
"You shut
up or I'm gonna put a screw through your chest."
Well,
I've,
I've never heard that expression.
I've been a DA since '68 and a criminal lawyer since '73.
I've just never heard the expression "put a screw through
 your chest."
And you're sort of
ambivalent about it.
On the one hand, you could kill the cop for this.
On the other hand,
you wish you could strangle your son
because he put himself in danger.
I mean, really, he was lucky he was in Westwood, in a
 public area
where he was not likely to get hit or something like that,
and it's sort of a naiveté for a seventeen-year-old at that
 time
to think that he's gonna be able to not
just watch out for himself.
So I said no way am I gonna get involved in the Rodney
 King case,

'cause I regarded it as a racial beating.
But what scares you—
it gives you pause when you find out how wrong you can be,
because you then
learn about an entire
historic event
and realize
that it's been misperceived.
Even Clinton,
who I like,
he got up on that morning and says, "Justice has finally been
    done."
How does he know?
What does he mean by justice?
Is he assuming that they're guilty?
Very strange, uh,
and I probably would have said the same thing if I was in
    his
position,
and I know,
I think I know what happened out there.
I mean,
I think,
I was certainly glad that Ted,
I was certainly glad that we escaped.
If you ask it more blatantly:
Is it better that two
innocent men get convicted
than that fifty innocent people die?
What is the answer to that?
I find the ambiguity . . .

I recognize it for what it is
and I'm willing to face it.
I've never,
that's why,
I've never used the Bible very much before.
I used it in my closing statement.
I actually have a Bible right here.
I'll see if I can find it for you.
I didn't read from the Bible, I referred to it.
Gotta remember.
It was the Saturday
after Good Friday and before Easter.
It's Matthew.
My father's an Orthodox Jew.
My mother is a Catholic,
so I was raised a Catholic.
In my closing statement
I used the parts of the Bible
from the trial of Christ,
because, really,
Pontius Pilate
wasn't such a bad sort.
He,
you know, he asked the right questions.
First he asked,
"What evil has this man done?"
And in Matthew,
where he focused on the individual guilts of a prisoner—
I'm referring to Christ as the prisoner
because I don't want this to become a theological thing—
and in Matthew,

Pontius Pilate
talks about
there being rioting in the city.
It's clear that Pontius Pilate
is trying to balance the fact that this man has done no evil
against the fact that there would be public disorder
if this man wasn't condemned.
And he wouldn't condemn him himself,
he had other people condemn him.
Can't find it.
Guess I have to send it to you.
Then in John
(He is still flipping through the Bible)
Pontius Pilate jested,
he says,
"What is truth?"
And it's a haunting question here too,
isn't it?
Is it the truth of Koon and Powell being guilty
or is it the truth of the society
that has to find them
guilty in order to protect itself?

Swallowing the Bitterness

Mrs. Young-Soon Han Former

liquor store owner

(A house on Sycamore Street in Los Angeles just south of Beverly. A tree-lined street. A quiet street. It's in an area where many Hasidic Jews live as well as yuppie types. Mrs. Young-Soon Han's living room is impeccable. Dark pink-and-apricot rug and sofa and chairs. The sofa and chairs are made of a velour. On the back of the sofa and chairs is a Korean design. A kind of circle with lines in it, a geometric design. There is a glass coffee table in front of the sofa. There is nothing on the coffee table. There is a mantel with a bookcase, and a lot of books. The mantel has about thirty trophies. These are her nephew's. They may be for soccer. On the wall behind the sofa area, a series of citations and awards. These are her ex-husband's. They are civic awards. There are a couple of pictures of her husband shaking hands with official-looking people and accepting awards. In this area is also a large painting of Jesus Christ. There is another religious painting over the archway to the dining room. There are some objects hanging on the side of the archway. Long strips and oval shapes. It is very quiet. When we first came in, the television was on, but she turned it off.

(She is sitting on the floor and leaning on the coffee table. When she hits her hand on the table, it sounds very much like a drum. I am accompanied by two Korean-American graduate students from UCLA.)

Until last year
I believed America is the best.

I still believe it.
I don't deny that now
because I'm a victim,
but
as
the year ends in '92
and we were still in turmoil
and having all the financial problems
and mental problems.
Then a couple months ago
I really realized that
Korean immigrants were left out
from this
society and we were nothing.
What is our right?
Is it because we are Korean?
Is it because we have no politicians?
Is it because we don't
speak good English?
Why?
Why do we have to be left out?
(She is hitting her hand on the coffee table)
We are not qualified to have medical treatment.
We are not qualified to get, uh,
food stamp
(She hits the table once),
not GR
(Hits the table once),
no welfare
(Hits the table once).
Anything.

Many Afro-Americans
(*Two quick hits*)
who never worked
(*One hit*),
they get
at least minimum amount
(*One hit*)
of money
(*One hit*)
to survive
(*One hit*).
We don't get any!
(*large hit with full hand spread*)
Because we have a car
(*One hit*)
and we have a house.
(*Pause six seconds*)
And we are high taxpayers.
(*One hit*)
(*Pause fourteen seconds*)
Where do I finda [sic] justice?
Okay, Black people
probably
believe they won
by the trial?
Even some complains only half right?
justice was there.
But I watched the television
that Sunday morning,
early morning as they started.
I started watch it all day.

They were having party and then they celebrated,
all of South-Central,
all the churches.
They finally found that justice exists
in this society.
Then where is the victims' rights?
They got their rights.
By destroying innocent Korean merchants . . .
They have a lot of respect,
as I do,
for
Dr. Martin King?
He is the only model for Black community.
I don't care Jesse Jackson.
But
he was the model
of nonviolence.
Nonviolence?
They like to have hiseh [sic] spirits.
What about last year?
They destroyed innocent people.
(Five-second pause)
And I wonder if that is really justice
(And a very soft "uh" after "justice," like "justicah," but very
quick)
to get their rights
in this way.
(Thirteen-second pause)
I waseh swallowing the bitternesseh,
sitting here alone
and watching them.

They became all hilarious
(*Three-second pause*)
and, uh,
in a way I was happy for them
and I felt glad for them.
At leasteh they got something back, you know.
Just let's forget Korean victims or other victims
who are destroyed by them.
They have fought
for their rights
(*One hit simultaneous with the word "rights"*)
over two centuries
(*One hit simultaneous with "centuries"*)
and I have a lot of sympathy and understanding for them.
Because of their effort and sacrificing,
other minorities, like Hispanic
or Asians,
maybe we have to suffer more
by mainstream.
You know,
that's why I understand,
and then
I like to be part of their
'joyment.
But . . .
That's why I had mixed feeling
as soon as I heard the verdict.

I wish I could
live together
with eh [sic] Blacks,
but after the riots
there were too much differences.
The fire is still there—
how do you call it?—
igni . . .
igniting fire.
(She says a Korean phrase phonetically: "Dashi yun gi ga nuh")
It's still dere.
It canuh
burst out anytime.

Lucia

Gladis Sibrian Director, Farabundo
Martí National Liberation Front, USA

(Morning at the Mark Taper Forum in a rehearsal
hall. I am videotaping her. She wears black pants
and a beautiful white linen shirt. She is from El Salvador. She was a nun who became a revolution-
ary.)

When I was, um,
thirteen, fourteen
years old,
my, my, my uncle and my relatives would say,
"How can you change things in this country?
It's impossible.
Sixty years of military dictatorship.
How can you change that?
And you're thirteen years old!"
"Ha," they will say,
"you wouldn't change anything."
That was the question
also in my school.
How can we young people
change things around?
And one of the things we have
was faith,
convictions.
That we have power within ourselves,
that we can change things.
People will say we are idealistic,

romantic,
part of our age.
We believe that.
Of course,
in the process
people did die.
I had a nom de guerre,
name of guerre.
My name was Lucia,
so people would refer to
light.
Luce.
Lucia.
Light.
What happened here in LA, I
call it a social explosion.
And what we call an uprising,
it's much more organized, planned.
So what happened here was more
spontaneous.
On the one hand,
I was, I was, I was excited,
I was excited that people
didn't just
let it pass,
let it pass by.
That, that, what happened,
declaring innocent the police,
and this spark through Rodney King
became
that,

what we call
the *detonante*.
There is a bomb and you pull the cord?
Detonante.
That's why we call it a social explosion
when people can no longer take it—
the status quo.
But on the other hand, I was sad
because it was anarchical,
it was not in any way planned,
organized.
For me it was sad, the way that many people
will die
without even knowing why they die.
Every day
in this Los Angeles
so many people die
and they didn't even know why they die.
There is no sense of future,
sense of hope
that things can be changed.
Why?
Because they don't feel that they have the power
within themselves,
that they can change things.

Limbo/Twilight #2
Twilight Bey Organizer of gang
truce

(In a Denny's restaurant in a shopping center. Saturday morning, February 1993. He is a gang member. He is short, graceful, very dark skinned. He is soft-spoken and even in his delivery. He is very confident.)

Twilight Bey,
that's my name.
When I was
twelve and thirteen,
I stayed out until, they say,
until the sun come up.
Every night, you know,
and that was my thing.
I was a
watchdog.
You know, I stayed up in the neighborhood,
make sure we wasn't being rolled on and everything,
and when people
came into light
a what I knew,
a lot a people said,
"Well, Twilight, you know,
you a lot smarter and you have a lot more wisdom than
    those
twice your age."
And what I did, you know,

I was
at home writing one night
and I was writing my name
and I just looked at it and it came ta me:
"twi,"
abbreviation
of the word "twice."
You take a way the "ce."
You have the last word,
"light."
"Light" is a word that symbolizes knowledge, knowing,
wisdom,
within the Koran and the Holy Bible.
Twilight.
I have twice the knowledge of those my age,
twice the understanding of those my age.
So twilight
is
that time
between day and night.
Limbo,
I call it limbo.
So a lot of times when I've brought up ideas to my
    homeboys,
they say,
"Twilight,
that's before your time,
that's something you can't do now."
When I talked about the truce back in 1988,
that was something they considered before its time,
yet

in 1992
we made it
realistic.
So to me it's like I'm stuck in limbo,
like the sun is stuck between night and day
in the twilight hours.
You know,
I'm in an area not many people exist.
Nighttime to me
is like a lack of sun,
and I don't affiliate
darkness with anything negative.
I affiliate
darkness with what was first,
because it was first,
and then relative to my complexion.
I am a dark individual,
and with me stuck in limbo,
I see darkness as myself.
I see the light as knowledge and the wisdom of the world
    and
understanding others,
and in order for me to be a, to be a true human being,
I can't forever dwell in darkness,
I can't forever dwell in the idea,
of just identifying with people like me and understanding me
    and mine.
So I'm up twenty-four hours, it feels like,
and, you know,
what I see at nighttime
is,

like,
little kids
between the ages of
eight and eleven
out at three in the morning.
They beatin' up a old man on the bus stop,
a homeless old man.
You know,
I see these things.
I tell 'em, "Hey, man, what ya all doin'?
Whyn't ya go on home?
What ya doin' out this time of night?"
You know,
and then when I'm in my own neighborhood, I'm driving
    through and I
see the living dead, as we call them,
the base heads,
the people who are so addicted on crack,
if they need a hit they be up all night doin' whatever they
    have to do
to make the money to get the hit.
It's like gettin' a total dose
of what goes on in the daytime creates at night.

Time Line March 1991–October 1993

1991

March 3: Los Angeles Police officers beat, subdue, and arrest Rodney G. King. George Holliday, a resident of a nearby apartment, captures the beating on videotape and distributes it to CNN and other stations; it is soon seen around the world.

March 6: Police Chief Daryl F. Gates calls beating an "aberration." Community leaders call for Gates's resignation.

March 7: King is released after the district attorney's office announces there is not enough evidence to file criminal charges.

March 15: Four Los Angeles police officers—Sergeant Stacey C. Koon and officers Laurence M. Powell, Timothy E. Wind, and Theodore J. Briseno—are arraigned on felony charges stemming from the King beating.

March 16: A store security camera records the fatal shooting of fifteen-year-old Latasha Harlins, an African-American girl, by Korean-American Soon Ja Du in a South Los Angeles liquor store.

March 26: The four police officers charged in the King beating plead not guilty. Soon Ja Du is arraigned on one count of murder.

March 28: Records show that $11.3 million was paid to victims of police brutality by the city of Los Angeles in 1990 to resolve police abuse cases.

April 1: In response to the King beating, Mayor Tom Bradley appoints a commission, headed by former deputy secretary of state Warren Christopher, to investigate the Los Angeles Police Department.

April 4: The Los Angeles Police Commission places Gates on sixty-day leave.

April 5: The city council orders the reinstatement of Gates.

April 7: Gates takes disciplinary action against the four criminally charged officers. He fires probationary officer Timothy Wind and suspends the other three without pay.

May 10: A grand jury decides not to indict any of the nineteen officers who were bystanders at the beating. The police department later disciplines ten of them.

July 9: The Christopher Commission report is released; it suggests Gates and the entire Police Commission step down.

July 10: Gates strips Assistant Chief David D. Dotson of his command after he complained openly of the chief's record in disciplining officers.

July 16: The Police Commission orders Gates to reinstate Dotson.

July 22: Gates announces he will retire in 1992.

July 23: The State Second District Court of Appeal orders the trial of the four LAPD officers moved out of Los Angeles County.

September 30: The prosecution in the Soon Ja Du–Latasha Harlins trial begins its case.

October 1: The police commission approves the vast majority of the 129 reform recommendations issued by the Christopher Commission.

October 11: The jury in Soon Ja Du's case returns a verdict: Du is found guilty of voluntary manslaughter.

November 6: The Los Angeles City Council approves spending $7.1 million to settle claims of police brutality and excessive force. Total payments for the year exceed $13 million.

November 15: Compton Superior Court Judge Joyce A. Karlin sentences Soon Ja Du to five years probation, four hundred hours of community service, and a five-hundred-dollar fine for the shooting death of Latasha Harlins. State Senator Diane Watson said, "This might be the time bomb that explodes."

November 26: Judge Stanley M. Weisberg chooses Simi Valley in neighboring Ventura County as the new venue for the trial of the officers charged in the King beating.

November 29: LAPD officers fatally shoot a black man, prompting a standoff with more than one hundred residents of the Imperial Courts housing project in Watts.

1992

February 3: Pretrial motions begin in the trial of the four LAPD officers accused of beating Rodney King.

March 4: Opening arguments begin in the King trial. None of the twelve jurors is African-American.

March 17: Prosecuting attorneys rest in the King trial.

April 3: Officer Briseno testifies that King never posed a threat to the LAPD officers.

April 16: Willie L. Williams, police commissioner in Philadelphia, is named to succeed Gates.

April 23: Jury begins deliberations in the King trial.

April 29: The jury returns not-guilty verdicts on all charges except one count of excessive force against Officer Powell; a mistrial is declared on that count alone. The verdict is carried live on television. Over two thousand people gather for a peaceful rally at First AME Church in South-Central Los Angeles. Violence erupts. Police dispatches relay reports of head wounds, vandalism, and burglary in an ever-widening radius. Reginald Denny is yanked from his truck cab and beaten unconscious at the intersection of Florence and Normandie; the incident is captured on video. Mayor Bradley declares a local emergency. Governor Pete Wilson calls out the National Guard. Fires break out over twenty-five blocks of central Los Angeles.

April 30: Bradley imposes a curfew for the entire city, restricts the sale of gasoline, and bans the sale of ammunition. The Justice Department announces it will resume an investigation into possible civil rights violations in the King beating. Retail outlets are looted and/or burned in South Los Angeles, Koreatown, Hollywood, Mid-Wilshire, Watts, Westwood, Beverly Hills, Compton, Culver City, Hawthorne, Long Beach, Norwalk, and Pomona.

May 1: More than a thousand Korean-Americans and others gather at a peace rally at Western Avenue and Wilshire Boulevard.

May 2: Clean-up crews hit the streets and volunteers truck food and clothing into the hardest hit neighborhoods. Thirty thousand people march through Koreatown in support of beleaguered merchants, calling for peace between Korean-Americans and blacks. Mayor Bradley appoints Peter Ueberroth to head the Rebuild LA effort. President Bush declares Los Angeles a disaster area.

May 3: The *Los Angeles Times* reports 58 deaths; 2,383 injuries; more than 7,000 fire responses; 12,111 arrests; 3,100 businesses damaged. The South Korean Foreign Ministry announces it will seek reparations for Korean-American merchants who suffered damages during the unrest.

May 4: With troops guarding the streets, Los Angeles residents return to work and school. Twenty to forty thousand people have been put out of work because their places of business were looted or burned. In violation of long-standing policy, LAPD officers cooperate with the Immigration and Naturalization Service and begin arresting illegal immigrants suspected of riot-related crimes. Suspects are turned over to the INS for probable deportation.

May 6: President Bush receives a telegram from Representative Dana Rohrabacher (Republican, Huntington Beach) demanding quick deportation of illegal immigrants arrested during the riots.

May 8: Federal troops begin to pull out from Los Angeles. The Crips and Bloods (the two major gangs in Los Angeles) announce plans for a truce.

May 11: Los Angeles Board of Police Commissioners appoints William H. Webster, former director of both the FBI and the CIA, to head a commission to study the LAPD's performance during the civil unrest.

May 12: Damian Williams, Antoine Miller, and Henry K. Watson are arrested for the beating of Reginald Denny on April 29. Gary Williams surrenders to police later that day. They quickly become known as the L.A. Four.

May 16: Led by mayors of many of the nation's largest cities, tens of thousands of protesters demonstrate in the nation's capital demanding billions of federal dollars in vast urban aid.

May 19: A mistrial is declared in the case of a Compton police officer accused of fatally shooting two Samoan brothers a total of nineteen times, mostly in their backs. The jury was deadlocked nine to three in favor of acquittal.

May 21: Damian Williams, Henry K. Watson, and Antoine Miller are arraigned on thirty-three charges for offenses against thirteen motorists at the intersection of Florence and Normandie, including the attack on Reginald Denny. Bail is set at $580,000 for Williams, $500,000 for Watson, and $250,000 for Miller. None is able to post bail.

May 25: Korean grocers and leaders from the Bloods and Crips meet to discuss an alliance.

May 30: Chief Gates steps down. Willie Williams is sworn in.

July 7: Korean-American protesters are pelted with office supplies tossed from city hall windows during seventeenth day of protests over poor treatment from government officials since the riots.

September 24: Mayor Tom Bradley announces that he will not seek reelection the following June.

October 17: The Webster Commission reports that deficiencies in the LAPD leadership led to failure to respond quickly to April's civil unrest.

November 10: The trial date for defendants in the Reginald Denny beating is set for March 15, 1993.

November 17: The Black-Korean Alliance members vote to disband.

December 14: The intersection of Florence and Normandie flares again as the Free the L.A. Four Defense Committee protests at the site of Denny's beating.

1993

January 22: Superior Court Judge John W. Ouderkirk dismisses ten charges against the defendants in the L.A. Four case, including charges of torture and aggravated mayhem. The charges of attempted murder stand.

February 3: The federal civil rights trial against the four police officers begins.

April 7: Judge Ouderkirk grants the defense in the Reginald Denny case additional time for preparation.

April 17: The verdicts are returned in the federal King civil rights trial. Officers Briseno and Wind are acquitted. Officer Powell and Sergeant Koon are found guilty of violating Rodney King's civil rights.

May 21: Peter Ueberroth resigns as cochairman of Rebuild L.A.

August 4: Sergeant Koon and Officer Powell are each sentenced to thirty-month prison terms.

August 19: The much-anticipated Reginald Denny beating trial begins in Los Angeles. Damian Williams, twenty, and Henry K. Watson, twenty-nine, are charged with a list of crimes including attempted murder of Reginald Denny and others in South Central near the corner of Florence and Normandie.

September 28: Final arguments begin in the Denny trial.

October 11: Judge Ouderkirk dismisses a juror for "failing to deliberate as the law defines it." The juror is replaced with an alternate.

October 12: Judge Ouderkirk removes a second juror, who asked to be excused for personal reasons, from the jury in the Reginald Denny trial.

October 18: Damian Williams and Henry Keith Watson are acquitted of many of the counts against them.

December 7: Damian Williams sentenced to a maximum of ten years in prison for attacks on Reginald Denny.

Excerpted from the Center Theatre Group/Mark Taper Forum program. The program was edited by Ken Werther and the time line was originally compiled by Mara Issacs and subsequently revised by the McCarter Theatre in Princeton, New Jersey. Reprinted with permission.

About the Author

Actress, playwright, and performance artist **Anna Deavere Smith** is the Obie Award winning writer-performer of *Fires in the Mirror: Crown Heights, Brooklyn, and Other Identities* (runner-up for the 1992 Pulitzer Prize in drama). The recipient of numerous other theater awards and honors, she is associate professor of drama at Stanford University.